RUDOLF LABAN

THE UNIVERSITY OF
WINCHESTER

D1610260

To be returned on or before the day marked above, subject to recall.

RUDOLF LABAN
Man of Theatre

Valerie Preston-Dunlop

DANCE BOOKS

DVDs of four of the works discussed in this book,
Recreating Rudolf Laban's Die Grünen Clowns,
Recreating Rudolf Laban's Nacht,
Recreating Rudolf Laban's Der Schwingende Tempel,
Recreating Rudolf Laban's Solos,
are available for purchase from the Dance Books web site:
www.dancebooks.co.uk

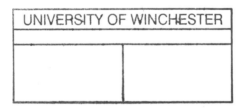

First published in 2013 by Dance Books Ltd.,
Southwold House, Isington Road, Binsted, Hampshire, GU34 4PH

© Valerie Preston-Dunlop

ISBN: 978-1-85273-167-0
A CIP catalogue for this title is available from the British Library

Printed in Great Britain

Contents

Introduction

Rudolf Laban is most well known as a theorist of movement and dance through his name being attached to methodologies of movement analysis and dance notation, Labananalysis and Labanotation. His preferred name for both was the more inclusive term choreology, first used in his research studio the *Choreographisches Institut* in 1926. He titled his institute to cover the dual meaning of writing a dance on paper in a script and authoring a dance in practice as a choreographer. Choreology and choreography were for him two sides of the same coin since his whole endeavour was to promote the integration of theory and practice of expressive movement in all its forms.

This book focuses on the neglected side of the man, his experimental dance theatre work and particularly on his creative methods. His main choreographic work was undertaken in Germany between 1912 to 1936, the year in which he was dismissed by his National Socialist employers. With his schools, books and notation forbidden, virtually all trace of his practice disappeared. As Norbert Servos puts it in the Introduction to his book on Pina Bausch's *Tanztheater*,

> Our own *Ausdruckstanz* tradition with names like Mary Wigman, Rudolf von Laban, Harald Kreutzberg and Gret Palucca had been all but dead since World War II.

His next point makes clear that the post war dance world in Germany was hesitant to re-engage.

> Striving for an apolitical supposedly timeless theater people avoided confrontation with the provocative ancestors...

But by 1984:

> Now for the first time, with Pina Bausch, contact was being re-established – albeit indirectly – with the almost forgotten revolutionary tradition.[1]

With the international success of Bausch's work, made more poignant now through her recent death, it seems timely to revisit the one 'provocative ancestor' who was the acknowledged leader of *Ausdruckstanz* [2] and to discuss ways of engaging with the dances that were thought to be lost. Alfred Schlee, the respected publisher and critic, referred to the expressionist dance form as *Der Neue Tanz* in his article in the journal *Schrifttanz* in 1930. Schlee's article

---

1 Servos, Norbert. *Pina Bausch Wuppertal Dance Theater or The Art of Training a Goldfish.* Cologne:Ballett-Bühnen-Verlag.1984.

2 Bausch's teacher at the *Folkwanghochschule* was Kurt Jooss, Jooss being a pupil and then collaborator with Laban for almost ten years.

is entitled, in translation, as 'The Turning Point of the New Dance'.[3]

> The New Dance was the most powerful manifestation of Expressionism. The Expressionist artist emphasised the immediacy of the work of art. He abhorred the idea of any form of intermediary which might thrust itself in between the inspiration and the realisation.

In the discussion in this book of the recreation process it will become clear how strong is the immediacy for the participating dancers in an expressionist work. In Schlee's informed opinion the most powerful period of *Ausdruckstanz* was in the early 1920s.

> The climax of the New Dance movement was reached in its first few years. Its energy was still unbroken, its achievements were magnificent.

To re-find that achievement has been my aim since I first became aware of the extent of Laban's output, and of his influence in Germany in the 1920s. To that end I, with the help of colleagues at the renowned training centre for professional musicians and dancers, Trinity Laban Conservatoire of Music and Dance, have located and recreated a sample of his works, performed them, filmed them, had documentaries made about them and now published this text, to make it possible for Laban's achievements to be revisited by the dance community and the public at large.

Schlee's comments confirm my selection of the works we have recreated, all from the first few years of the New Dance, which continued until 1939, with *Der Schwingende Tempel* from 1922, the *Kammertanz Solos and Duos* from 1924, *Nacht* from 1927 and *Die Grünen Clowns* from 1928.[4]

In a later paragraph in his article Schlee states:

> The New Dance is obstinate. It does not concede to only having been an episode.

Indeed Laban had great difficulty in coming to terms with the vogue for 'the new objectivity', the *Neue Sachlichkeit,* that began to replace the subjectivity of Expressionism and led to the reification of the dancer, Oskar Schlemmer's photogenic *Triadic Ballet* being the strongest example. It was Laban's erstwhile pupil Kurt Jooss who took *Ausdrucktanz* forward, underlined by his success in the International Choreographic Competition of 1932 with his masterpiece *Der Grüne Tisch* (The Green Table). Laban as president of the jury acknowledged Jooss's supremacy while Laban himself was struggling with an uncooperative ballet company at the Berlin Opera.

---

3 Preston-Dunlop, V. & Lahusen, S. eds. *Schrifttanz: A View of Dance in the Weimar Republic.* London: Dance Books. 1990.

4 The following DVDs offer visual documentaries and films of these performances. *Recreating Rudolf Laban's Der Schwingende Tempel 1922,* Cheltenham; IDM Ltd. *Recreating Rudolf Laban's Kammertanz Solos and Duos,* London: Vitafilms. *Recreating Rudolf Laban's Nacht 1927,* Cheltenham: IDM Ltd. 2013. *Recreating Rudolf Laban's Die Grünen Clowns 1928.*Cheltenham: IDM Ltd 2010.

This book presents Laban through a chapter outlining the influences in his life and context that affected his making of theatre works. Since he was a man acutely engaged with his surrounding culture and making works that commented on it I have had to include his time as a military cadet, his studies in architecture, his Symbolist art teachers, his Rosicrucian belief system, his living in cities vibrant with changes in art, the Paris of *Les Fauves*, Munich and the emergence of Abstract Expressionism, Zurich and Dada, Germany and Expressionism. The decadence of *fin de siècle* Paris, the political and financial turmoil of the Weimar Republic are embedded in his works and are discussed.

One chapter presents the archival resources that I have located and are available for anyone to study, followed by chapters on the recreations of significant works in his repertoire. The recreation process, the work's conceptual base and context and the practical studio work of each choreography are presented and discussed by a team of artist-researchers all participating in the realisation of these performances. This text follows the search for Laban's forgotten works and looks at the kinds of evidence needed for a performance of such an ephemeral art form. The discovery of Laban's singular methods of treating major choreographic events as a form of practical research is presented while his smaller works are treated as typical expressionist immediacy.

This project has highlighted issues for dance scholarship, in particular for practitioners as historians. In so many cases the dance community divides itself into those who dance and those who talk about it as if they live in separate worlds. Having been brought up myself in the Laban tradition where there is no distinction made between practice and theory, both operate in the moment of creative dancing, it has always seemed unsurprising to me that as a dance scholar I am as at home in the library and archive as I am in the studio. That perspective is intrinsic in the training of dancers at Trinity Laban and their capacities have contributed to our ability to mount these works with integrity. My dance collaborators Alison Curtis-Jones and more recently Melanie Clarke are steeped in choreological and choreographic practice. Our composer colleagues Oli Newman and Robert Coleridge compose and play for the recreations within the *Ausdruckstanz* concept that dance must be primary with the music supporting it. That requires the composer to wait until the choreography is emerging and work in response to it.

Alfred Schlee points to a reality that most artistic movements include:

> [Expressionism's] radicalism can only be understood as a reaction to what went on before.

For Laban's revolutionary working methods what went on before in German dance, and continued to go on, was ballet 'at a very low ebb', as Schlee puts it. Laban's encounter with that low ebb was in his uncomfortable attempts to work with the ballet troupes of city opera houses. But what went on before and during Laban's creative period is also a matter of *Zeitgeist* or rather the changing spirit of the times that the tumultuous world events of early 20th century brought about and Laban's *Weltanschauung,* his personal philosophy. These are issues that the recreator as practical historian has to engage with.

Was it only the appalling political events of the Nazi period that annihiliated Laban from history or is the art form's ephemerality a contributing factor to its disappearance? History is largely transmitted through words and images on paper. While plenty of words have been researched and recorded in my biography of Laban and Evelyn Dörr's writing[5] to complement Laban's own autobiography, the visual images are sparse, in sepia and often staged as a photocall. Compared with painting and sculpture whose art works are permanent and well-photographed, dance, the ephemeral art, is profoundly difficult to write about in a way that conjures what was really there. It explains the poverty of critical discourse on dance as 'the most powerful manifestation of Expressionism' in the cultural histories of the period. It has contributed to the neglect of Laban as a man of theatre. A.V. Coton, writing on *Kurt Jooss and his Work* in 1946 was of the opinion:

> Laban is one of the little-appreciated thinkers in the last fifty years of theatrical history; it is probable that he will be reckoned as historically important as Delsarte, Appia and Stanislavsky. [6]

Perhaps this text and the visual recordings of the recreations might enable readers today to judge for themselves.

5 Preston-Dunlop, V. *Rudolf Laban: An Extraordinary Life.* London: Dance Books. 1998. Dörr, E. *Rudolf Laban: The Dancer of the Crystal.* Plymouth. The Scarecrow Press. 2008.
6 Coton, A.V. *The New Ballet.* London: Dennis Hobson. 1946.

Chapter One
Rudolf Laban, the man and his culture

No attempt is made here to give a full account of Laban's life but rather of his theatre work, and because he responded so strongly and directly to the events occurring around him this chapter is much more than a statement of what he made when and with whom. His autobiography, published in Germany in 1935, provides another view, a striking background to his aspirations, anxieties and thoughts covering his most active period of dance making.[1] Divided in chapters each of which is entitled by one of his major choreographic works it is a much-used source for this book. My biography of the man covers all aspects of Laban's output for he was a polymath. It encompasses his books, articles, notation, works for amateur dancers, his struggles with administration, his research, his personal life as lover and father, his continual lack of money, his poor health and bipolar personality as well as his theatre work.[2] Evelyn Dörr's doctoral thesis traces Laban's life and work drawing on the archives available to her primarily in Leipzig and Berlin and is a useful source on the documentation of his performances.[3] The recent *Laban Sourcebook*, edited by Dick McCaw makes available selected translations and commentaries on Laban's writings.[4] These useful sources are supplemented by archive holdings and I discuss their relevance to his dance theatre in the next chapter.

This chapter traces the essential influences on the man and decisions made by him divided into periods connected with the cities in which he lived. Later chapters on the recreations of his choreographic works that we have undertaken focus on four moments, the three dances presented together in 1922, the chamber dances of 1924, the three works presented in 1927 and the satire in 1928. These chapters give an insider view on specific works written by the collaborators who have recreated them for today's audiences.

---

1 Laban, R. *Ein Leben für den Tanz*, 1935. Trans. Lisa Ullmann as *A Life for Dance*. London. Macdonald and Evans. 1975.

2 Preston-Dunlop, V. *Rudolf Laban: An Extraordinary Life*. London. Dance Books. 1998.

3 Dörr, E. *Rudolf von Laban: Leben und Werk des Künsters, 1979–1936*. Unpublished PhD thesis, 1999. Extended as his lifestory *Rudolf Laban: The Dancer of the Crystal*, with translation assistants Lori Ann Lantz, Amy J. Klemment. Plymouth: Scarecrow Press.2008

4 McCaw, D. Ed. *The Laban Sourcebook*. London: Routledge. 2011.

1879 – 1900

Bratislava and Budapest, his childhood

Rudolf Jean Baptist Attilla Laban de Varalja was born in what is now Bratislava, capital of Slovakia. At the time of his birth Bratislava was in the Austro-Hungarian Empire, and Laban's father was a General directing the army of occupation in the Balkans. The family spoke Hungarian and French, and German when in Vienna, the city of culture no more than an hour away. The boy was educated in Budapest and the grammar school in Bratislava. Apart from his obligatory studies he was taught to paint, to play the piano, and he attended opera performances and made his own *tableaux vivants* for celebratory events in the city.

Cities were awash with dance in those days, people danced every day, for fun, to celebrate anything. It was normal for boys and girls to dance, picking up the steps and forms of the local style. Laban ran a prize-winning boys'group of Czardas dancers as a teenager.

His uncle designed the new city theatre in Bratislava and through him the boy had access backstage. He assisted in painting backcloths, was a familiar figure at the stage door and became both attracted to the possibilities of theatre and repelled by its artificiality and contrasts, the bejeweled Queen of the Night contrasted with the 'wretched' chorus singer.

> The stage of the future – for me already a dethroned queen of the night – had to be something quite different. It must be a healthy festival of joy in the clear sunlight of daytime, without these pretenses and trappings which smother all the essentials.[5]

This idealist view of theatre of a young man never left him entirely but what Laban retained was that something new had to happen and that he had the vision to make it happen.

Sarajevo, Wiener Neustadt and Istanbul

For many school holidays the boy joined his father, stationed near Sarajevo/ Herzegovina. From twelve years old he was a military cadet seeing army life at first hand, encountering the tension between the Turkish and Slav communities. He became an excellent horseman and fencer, learned all manner of martial arts, and admired military discipline and the movement of thousands of men in military manoevres and ceremonial tattoos. **1.1**

On one occasion his father's duties took him to Istanbul. Laban went with him and witnessed an event that had a huge influence on his choosing dance as a career. He saw a Mevlevi Dervish ritual, and sword dance. The Dervish Moslem brothers are well known for their trance-inducing whirling,

5 Laban, 1935, p. 32.

less known for the ritual dances in which they pierce the skin of their arms and chests with swords as they dance for long periods, blood flowing, at the end of which the wounds disappear and are completely healed. This 'magic' overwhelmed Laban. He wrote years later this simple question:

> Could dancing really have such a power over men?[6]

The sense that dance did indeed have power, have an impressive as well as an expressive function, informed many aspects of his career, particularly his championing of dance for all, what we might call community dance, and his focus on his audiences and the effect that his theatre work had on them.

It was in the wild countryside of the Balkans that his first projected movement work *Die Erde* (The Earth) came to his mind, consisting in a Song of the Animal, a Song of the Plant, a Song of the Crystal and a Song of Man. His imagination ran riot. Of the animal he wrote:

> Now I knew how both courage and greed towered in its soul like an unyielding rock; how its death pounce was like lightning and its roar like a howling storm.

On exploring a deep gorge he wrote:

> Suddenly the cutting widens, but it gets no lighter because everywhere the thickly matted plants cast a deep shade over the water. Branches of huge trees twist into one another, parasitic plants coil luxuriantly around them. The musty air takes on a sickly sweet flavour. Complete silence reigns. Here live the plants, plants by themselves, for themselves, greedy and self-indulgent... the mighty in-drawing, craving thirst of its soul. Earth, how terrible are your children!

The third song was to the

> "Resounding crystal
> Icy life of stone"

> which became for me the symbol of the discerning ingenious spirit of nature; as the plant became the impulses of the life of feeling, of all the stirrings of emotion. The animal is, however, the strongest archetype of that tremendous will and dynamic force which fills the whole of nature.

Of the fourth song he wrote:

> Man is the promise of the earth if he has the strength to unite the three elemental forces and bring them to the highest point of development. [7]

He would return to *Die Erde* on Monte Verita years later where sections of it were worked through creatively with his group, linking poetry with dance.[8]

---

6 Laban 1935, p. 52.

7 Laban 1935, pp 22, 23, 26.

8 Mary Wigman gives a vivid account of their workshops on *Die Erde* in 'Rudolf Labans Lehre vom Tanz' in *Die neue Schaubühne*. Sep 1921, pp. 99 – 106.

From this world of imagination he returned to the real world. To achieve his father's wish that he should follow him into the army, the young man was enrolled into the military academy at Wiener Neustadt to train as an officer. Two events there were significant to his career. Struck by the adoration for militarism and military hardware by everyone around him, he had what one can only call a moment of clairvoyance.

> I saw with growing clarity how man will come under the domination of the machine... Thrilling as the power of conquest over air and sea might be, man will clearly have to pay dearly for it... Wasn't the magic word 'Soul'? But hadn't the soul already withered and died in the maze of our spurious culture in the turmoil of the big city? Wasn't it irreparably and irretrievably lost? Wasn't it the task of the arts to re-awaken it, to keep it alive? And didn't I belong much more to those whose task it was to arouse the soul through their dreams and prayers than those who increased the power of the machine...?[9]

The second was a celebration that he organised partly in a rebellious spirit against militarism. He dragooned his fellow cadets into putting on a festival celebrating the indigenous dances from the areas that they came from.

> The German waltz... the magnificent Hungarian Czardas...the Slovakian circle dance the Kolo... Poles with their Mazurka... the Bohemians their polka, the Styrians landler, the Tyrolese their schuplattler, an Italian tarantella... Ruthenian Russian dance and Herzegovinian dervish.

Although his training for a career in dance was not traditional, he was clearly very knowledgeable about and skilled in this aspect of dance.

Laban abandoned the military academy, to the devastation of his father, made his decision to become an artist of some sort and enrolled in the Écoles des Beaux Arts in Paris in the school of architecture.

1900-1912

Paris and Munich

Before studying in Paris Laban had taken painting instruction for a few months from Herman Obrist in Munich. Obrist was a visionary, drawing the images of his dreams on waking and transforming them into embroideries. His belief in a spiritual layer to human life was not unusual. At the end of the 19th century Theosophy was a growing interest as the validity of institutional religious practices were questioned. Laban's youthful interest in a spiritful world was fuelled by Obrist. When Laban arrived in Paris he was ready for the Rosicrucian cell that he found at the Écoles. **1. 2**

Much could be said about Rosicrucianism in Paris but the essential for the discussion of Laban's theatre work is that his overriding philosophy

---

9 Laban 1935, p. 48, 49.

that informed the decisions of his adult life stem from Rosicrucianism encountered first here. The Rosicrucian scholar Christopher McIntosh:

> I believe that the most fruitful way to look at Rosicrucianism is not as a specific doctrine of authority handed down through a succession of groups, but rather as the way that certain individuals have chosen to express an inner quest.[10]

An inner quest is certainly what Laban experienced. The Rosicrucian quest consists in tracing how human beings since time began have expressed their spiritual beliefs, tracing evidence in myths, songs, stories, signs and marks, rituals and dances. A Rosicrucian quest involves being aware of how present spirituality is expressed, including your own. At this point, in Paris, Laban had little idea just where his quest would lead him. Eventually he settled on dance and the expressive body as the area of his research but not yet. The Rosicrucian cell associated with the Écoles included, over several decades, painters and musicians including Gustave Moreau, Claude Debussy, Erik Satie and Henri Matisse, and the extraordinary figure of Sar Peladan who opened the Rose + Croix Salon where artists exhibited their work.

McIntosh continues:

> Every seeker after truth must choose the symbology that accords best with his own particular search.

In what form will the truth that is being sought be expressed? In religious rites? In poetry? By Paris Laban knew it was in the arts, he had suspicions that it might be dance but in reality a career in female dominated dance, dismissed as frivolous, for a man of his family background and expectations, was out of the question. Whatever art form he decided upon it would be 'questful', a search for inner truth to be found through that art. The Rosicrucian quest was not only for knowledge but had the anticipation that something new was imminent, a time of change, hope and spiritual renewal. This quest is the underlying topic of his 1922 dance theatre piece *Der Schwingende Tempel* (The Swinging Temple) whose recreation is discussed in a later chapter.

At the Écoles des Beaux Arts Laban will have been drawn into the group that had studied with the symbolist painter Gustave Moreau until his death in 1898. They were painters, several of them members of the Rosicrucian cell. Moreau had taught a freedom with colour advocating colour as more significant than the object it represented. When these painters, later led by Henri Matisse, saw a touch of red in a still life object they painted it with vermillion, a suggestion of blue in a landscape was painted ultramarine, a suspicion of sunlight was painted in broad bright yellow strokes. They became known as *Les Fauves* (The Beasts) for their stark colours thrown onto the page. Laban's own paintings in Paris do not appear to be influenced but his later movement does in that his range of dynamics compared with the

---

10 McIntosh, C. *The Rosicrucians*. Boston: Weiser Books. 1998, p.139.

range of ballet is intense. He was not afraid of going to the extremes of *Les Fauves* as the photographs of his 'flying and falling' training sessions of the men and women in his *Tanzbühne* in 1921 show. **(see 3.5** in Chapter 3**)**

Les Fauves developed into, or was subsumed into, Expressionism, the art movement that became almost all-embracing lasting well into the 1920s. Painters, actors, dancers, playwrights, turned to how the soul might express itself directly as paint on to the canvas, as words onto the page, as the dynamic body in space. German expressionism was particularly strong and in Alfred Schlee's opinion the New Dance led by Laban was 'the most powerful manifestation of it'.[11] It was an experiential art, the artist's experience of 'rapturous force' went onto the canvas, what the dancer experienced as 'ecstasy' became the performance.[12] But in Paris Laban was not yet ready for this responsibility.

His architecture studies were invaluable to his future career. He studied proportion, density of materials, a 3D perspective and geometry all of which appear in his writings on the grammar of movement, particularly in *Choreographie* (1926) and *Choreutics* (1966). He undertook still life, landscape studies and life drawing. Observing people became a fascination to him. We know he studied the patients in the asylum for the insane near where he lived with his wife and his caricatures and cartoons were drawn from sharp observation. It looks as if they were influenced by Aubrey Beardsley in style. Alistair Duncan wrote this of Beardsley:

> [His notoriety arose] from the macabre character of his subject matter. His renderings evoked life's more sinister aspects, those which Victorian society deemed taboo: perversion, eroticism, corruption and depravity.[13]

Everything Beardsley stood for was anathema to Laban. So was his aping of Beardsley done in the spirit of capturing all that he despised in city life as he did in the theatre work *Nacht*, a critique of 'the adoration of dollars, deceit and depravity'?

Laban's architecture studies ended with his examination for the Prix de Rome. He failed in company with two thirds of the applicants. The task in 1903 was to design a city theatre. Laban produced a radical theatre in the round, with no proscenium arch, quite possibly influenced by Obrist. It was not only radical aesthetically and structurally but embodied his growing socialist inclinations. He designed no prestigious sections in his theatre, every seat had an equal view of the event that would in any case have to be directed 'in the round' which is not what city theatre directors were ready

11 Schlee, A. trans as 'At the turning point of the New Dance'. *Schrifttanz* Vol. III. no. 1, April 1930, in Preston-Dunlop, V. and Lahusen, S. eds. *Schrifttanz: A View of German Dance in the Weimar Republic*. London: Dance Books, 1990.

12 Lucie-Smith, E. *Symbolist Art*. London: Thames and Hudson. 1972, p.7.

13 Duncan, A. *Art Nouveau*. London. Thames and Hudson. 1994, p.20.

for at that time. His theatre would obviously be ideal for the kind of dance performances that he was beginning to envisage. **1.3**

In Paris the young man was given a letter of introduction to a 'fashionable poet', a distant cousin, we do not know who he was, who introduced him to the salon culture of 'Madame X'. Laban devoted pages to his description of this 'Queen of the Night 'and her circle of fawning dandies and the despicable places of amusement where the Parisian rich took their pleasure and to which the Queen took him. The contrast between the casual depravity of the wealthy and the shocking poverty of the working man and woman on whom they depended, the waiter, the doorman, the shop girl, devastated Laban. What he described was the basis of *Nacht*, everything he loathed. The chapter on our recreation of *Nacht* discusses this episode in detail.

In biographical notes on Laban written by his associate Albrecht Knust, we learn that Laban 'studied classical ballet at the Paris Opera'.[14] Just what that amounted to is not known but that he knew classical ballet sufficiently to analyse it in his book *Choreographie* (1926) is clear. While ballet informed his development of the notation he turned his back on it completely for his theatre work. He deliberately contrasted with the elements of ballet's vocabulary, ballet's relationship between dancer and choreographer, and the hierarchic structure of a ballet company.

While in Paris Laban married Martha Fricke, a fellow student with whom he had two children. Their idyllic life was shattered in 1907 when Martha died, never recovering from the second birth. Laban was devastated. Martha's parents took the children while Laban fell to his first severe bout of depression, returning to his parents' house in Vienna.

Munich 1910

Munich was the arts centre of Germany as the second decade of the 20th century began, with Schwabing its artists' quarter. In 1910 Laban decided to restart his career there with his new wife, singer Maja Lederer. His skill as a graphic designer gave him opportunity to earn in the city's businesses and the Carnival season offered him the chance to direct celebratory events. Lisa Ullmann described the atmosphere thus:

> Munich, before WW1, was the scene not only of the most lively and progressive thought in the arts in Europe but also a city which pursued its festivals with exuberant mirth. During Shrove-tide one great festival would follow hot on the heels of the other and artists and laymen took pride in preparing original decorations and spectacular performances. [15]

In his autobiography Laban devoted several pages to these 'frenzies'

---

14 Knust, A. *Vortrag Albrecht Knust 21.5.32.* unpublished. Laban Collection.

15 Laban 1935, fn p.77.

providing his reader with a glimpse of the mayhem of directing eight hundred men and women in a 'witches-sabbath of the metropolis confronting a witches-sabbath of unspoilt nature', giants, demons, witches, dwarfs, dancing in a huge contraption, 'the jaws of hell' with stalagmite teeth. Then on to the next mayhem, this time for the medical community, with another huge cast and stage effects.

He had evidently gathered around him in Schwabing dancers and actors who became his assistants for these mammoth performances. He gained an enviable reputation. Although these events were not where his aspirations lay, they led to a kernel of collaborators and supporters who would enable him in 1912 to make the decision to devote his life to the renewal of dance.

In the Munich art world the *Blaue Reiter* group of painters led by Wassily Kandinsky was the voice to be heard. Kandinsky's early paintings were regarded as Symbolist, surfaces with a deeper layer of some sort. Kandinsky was exploring how that deeper layer might be brought to the surface.[16] Both Laban and he were attracted to the lectures of Rudolf Steiner, by then well known, who had developed his own spiritual path of Anthroposophy promoting a spirituality free from priests, gurus and religious dogmas with direct access to 'a deeper spiritual layer' of life by each individual. Steiner was also a Rosicrucian, at some point he led the Munich Lodge that Laban frequented.[17] The question began to be asked: how can we embody the spiritual in our art making? For Kandinsky this became his quest, to identify the spiritual in the very stuff a painting was made of, its colour and its form. He discussed his thoughts in his 1911 book *Über das Geistige in der Kunst* (Concerning the spiritual in art), giving birth as it were to Abstract Art. Since the painting came directly from the artist's experience to the canvas it was classified as Expressionist but of a particular sort, Abstract Expressionism.

Just who started the discussion of how to embody the spiritual in the *Bewegungskünst* (the movement arts) is not known but an answer came from two sources. In 1912 Marie Steiner proposed a new prayerful movement art, *Eurythmie*, by which vowel and consonant sounds are translated into a series of gestures so that great poetry or biblical sources might be 'danced'. It is 'visible speech, visible song'.[18] Eurythmy could not constitute an adequate movement art for the 20th century in Laban's view because it was derivative, and for Laban dance must become independent, a primary art. Eurythmy's dance was dependent on something else, in this case words. In the same summer Emile Jaques-Dalcrose's school of *Eurythmics* upped their art from being purely an education of the body through music to being an art form

---

16 Kandinsky's early teacher was Herman Obrist.

17 Rosicrucianism is seen as the 33rd degree of Freemasonry and their meeting place was the Masonic Lodge.

18 Steiner, R. *A Lecture on Eurhythmy.* London: Anthroposophical Publishing Co, 1926.

of performance through productions in their new purpose built home at Hellerau outside Dresden. They gave an interpretation of *Orfeo and Euridice* that became an internationally supported occasion. Laban was invited and witnessed the production. Maybe what tipped Laban was the paper Dalcrose published with it entitled 'How to revive dancing' in which he critiqued ballet and proposed a way forward for dance as music visualisation.[19]

In any event after this production Laban made his decision that his vision for the renewal of dance as dependent on nothing but itself, must be put into practice. From letters to Suzanne Perrottet, a Dalcrose teacher, with whom he started an affair, he wrote that he had put his drawings and paintings away. His art studio had become a dance studio. It was a brave move for he had with that decision not only to earn enough for his growing family through dance but to recognise that his life was not his own but the vehicle for a quest, a quest in dance.

1912-1918

Monte Verita, Munich and Zurich

Gathering round him a group from the Carnival celebrations he opened a school and commenced what one can only call practical research in what 'renewal of dance' might be. The first decision was clear for him, music must be removed. If dance were to become a primary art and not a derivative art of music then the music must be removed to reveal what dance itself was. What commenced was a tumult of experimentation in which the titles he chose for his work New Dance and Free Dance were literally that, freed from learnt vocabularies of steps, freed from the constraints of clothing, freed from the necessity of a story, freed from metric rhythm. He championed improvisation as a way of discovering new movement, new rhythms. At this point his architecture studies bore fruit. The idea of dance as living architecture brought in the crucial ingredient of space. Dalcrose's definition had been 'Dancing is the art of expressing emotion by means of rhythmic body movement' but for Laban dance was simply the dynamic body in space.[20]

For dance to stand on an equal footing with music it needed to have a valid theory equivalent to music's theory of harmony and rhythm. For it to have equal footing with painting, dance must have the equivalent to painting's theory of form and colour. Gradually he saw that dance functioned with

---

19 Jaques-Dalcrose, E. 'How to revive dancing (1912)' in *Rhythm, Music and Education.* Woking: The Dalcrose Society. 1921.

20 The correspondence with Perrottet is housed in the Kunsthaus Zurich, some of the letters appear in *Suzanne Perrottet: Ein Bewegtes Leben*. Ed Wolfensberger. Bern: Benteli. Verlag, undated (1990)

a harmonic system of spatial forms with all manner of symmetries and directions and a rich panoply of kinetic rhythms, dynamics and phrasing. These could be developed as comprehensive principles and practice and this he set out to do. He developed it over a ten year period into the comprehensive studies of Choreutics and Eukinetics.

The second decision was political. He knew from experience that dance would not be taken seriously if it remained a domain of women. He set about deliberately exploring the male element of movement and including material of that ilk in his classes, such elements as impactive rhythms as well as impulsive, forceful as well as delicate, combative as well as collaborative, angular as well as rounded. These materials went straight into his theatre works, into casting, into topics that appealed to men as well as women.

The third decision was also political. He felt that dance would not become a discussed and serious part of culture if it had no means of being studied by theorists and historians as other arts could because they were literate. The ephemerality of dance was double-edged in his view, providing a freedom for living-in-the-moment creativity but also a weakness in that that creativity disappeared as it was danced. You have to remember that filming dance was not yet possible. He set about studying existing dance notation systems and analysing movement in terms of how he might find new means for writing as a score the kind of fresh dance material that the 20th dance would produce. It was a formidable task that took more than a decade to complete.

His ever-returning depression hit after the high of getting things started and crucial decisions made. In a letter to Perrottet he wrote:

> Something is broken in me, I am not sure if it is illness or something else or if it is that after the mad work of this summer, I am in the necessity of leaving all that preoccupies me. What is worse is that I detest my ideas, I hate them, everything disgusts me, I don't see any way with which I could accomplish my ideas. Not enough talent, not enough knowledge, nor in music nor in painting – sad, sad is the song. [21]

Desperate for money he took on every bit of work in the Carnival frenzy of winter 12/13. Coming out of his depression he wrote to Perrottet about the musical composition experiments he was making as a complement to what he was discovering about dance:

> The poetry of tensions, the counterweight, the equilibrium, the constant changes in tensions, as well in soloists as the group – the exuberance of dimensional feeling, the brutality or feebleness of the driving force and the struggle between time and dimensions.[22]

---

21 Letter from Laban to Suzanne Perrottet, Oct 5 1912. (trans Simone Michelle). Laban Collection.

22 Laban to Perrottet March 1913.

He started to attract Dalcrose adherents. Amongst them was Marie Wiegmann (sic)[23] with her phenomenal talent who would prove an invaluable advocate before she developed her own career. With the support of dramaturge Hans Brandenburg, a man convinced that Laban had unique talent for the task he had set himself, he accepted an invitation to run a school for the arts at the alternative commune on Monte Verita (The Mountain of Truth) in the Ticino, for the summer months of 1913.

These six years, 1912-18, compounded by World War I, were extraordinary. The summer months of 1913 and 14 offered an idyllic setting with an atmosphere of experimentation and alternative living with the freedom and encouragement to try anything and everything organic and progressive. While the winter months back in Munich gave Laban the opportunity to study, give public lectures, get his school going, give the first performances, Monte Verita was where he tried out his first dance theatre ideas with no pressure. With his bipolar condition, at Monte Verita Laban was on a tumultuous high. By contrast the years in Zurich after WWI began were unrelenting struggle where also anything could happen and did but not to Laban's advantage.

He describes two dances or 'plays with a purpose' made at Monte Verita. *Ishtar's Journey to Hades* told the tale of the queen Ishtar who cast off her adornments at each stage of her journey into the underworld until she stood naked at the last gate.

> In my dance the worldly cast-off possessions were symbolised by Ishtar's followers. They were the vanities, the egoism and the vices of human beings, and one of them had to stay behind at each gate, until Ishtar passed through the last one alone. Thus she bade farewell to the crown of pride, the cloak of hypocrisy, the sceptre of violence, the necklace of vanity, the veil of selfishness, the girdle of cowardice.[24]

The event ended with a solemn dance where she was no longer a 'ruler but one of them'. The purpose of the dance was:

> an elementary example of how, through the power of the ideas expressed in our dances, I tried to induce my group to relinquish all the enticements of our civilisation. I hardly ever talked about these things.

The interest in *Ishtar* lay in the direct way Laban embodied an idea in movement. The body part to dominate the dance of each of Ishtar's followers is clear, the crown for the head, the cloak for the torso, the sceptre for the arms, and so on. He is not asking his dancers to imagine being proud or hypocritical but to create a dance around the possibilities of the head

---

23 Marie Wiegmann changed her name to Mary Wigman when she commenced her independent career in 1919.

24 Laban, 1935, p.86

and the torso. Another interest was in his development of an ensemble, deliberately non-hierarchic, that would become a hall mark of his *Tanzbühne* company. Ishtar ended her story no more important than her followers. Also interesting is his belief in the impressive power of dance. He did not tell his dancers what the dance meant, he expected and succeeded by all accounts that they knew through the osmosis of kinetic experience.

They created a sequence of dances entitled *The Dancing Drumstick*, a 'play-with-a-purpose' to develop his dancers' sense of rhythm, significant since many of them started with the music dependency of Dalcrose. His idea was that rhythmic patterns, danced and playing with all manner of eukinetic phrases of pace, force and metre are expressive in their own right of the 'inner stirrings' of the human heart, mind and spirit, and have always been so, with drummed messages being a way that indigenous people communicated. His study of early cultures as part of his Rosicrucian quest was no doubt the source of *The Dancing Drumstick*. Evelyn Dörr gives 'hand drums, tambourines, gongs, clappers, cymbals, castanets, wood blocks and flutes' as the percussion they worked with.

The Monte Verita school was a school for *TanzTon Wort und Plastik* (Dance, Sound, Word and the Plastic Arts) with Suzanne Perrottet soon assisting with sound and Maja Lederer with song and words. They danced outside on the grass, by the lakeside in very little clothing to feel the connection with the air around them, the breeze on their naked skin, the grass under their bare feet. **1.4** The whole experience was corporeal and sensual. They did everything themselves, grew food, cooked food, dug the earth, made costumes, lived in the most primitive huts. Käthe Wulff, a radical and political woman who joined the group, lived in a large cardboard box, so she told me. Anything went, including the mores of sexual and middle-class behaviour. Everything was taken to the extreme. The image included is one of a group of photographs by Johan Adam Meisenbach, many of which have the dancers without clothing.

That space became more than itself for the Laban school was first noted in the press of 1919 in reviews of Mary Wigman's performances, but was clearly started here at Monte Verita. As Laban's study of dance as living architecture proceeded, the geometry of space became a focus. After all patterns in space are what geometry is and patterns in space are what dance is. From his Rosicrucian studies he was familiar with Plato's view of the cosmos and of number and what are known as 'the platonic solids', the tetrahedron, octahedron, cube, icosahedron and dodecahedron. These fundamental geometric forms had deeply spiritual connections, for Plato, with the elements earth, air, fire and water. That symbolism was not Laban's interest but he decided to explore the fundamental idea that a regular geometric form might have significance of some sort for dance. If you want to study a series of patterns you need a grid against which to study their detail. He needed a three dimensional grid of the kinesphere, the sphere surrounding each dancer, against which to study patterns of gestures and moves. In Laban's view the human being uses an unacknowledged grid of the space surrounding each one to help them be aware of the patterns they make. He went on to investigate through trial and error with Mary Wigman, what the grid of human behavioural and expressive movement might be. What is the grid of fencing, he asked, what is the grid of interpersonal gestures or grid of the ballet's port de bras? The questions poured out of him and eventually he came to see from his observations that the cube was the grid of the place we are in, with its walls and ceiling, and the icosahedron was the grid most akin to the human skeletal condition of vertical symmetry and gestures that are curved.[25] **1.5**

For dance at Monte Verita each dancer's kinesphere took its place in the space shared with other people and, more widely, in the cosmos. Dancing outside in nature this can be a direct experience, as you lift up you address the cosmos, as you drop down you connect to the earth, as you open and move across horizontally you reach to the horizon, moving forwards you connect with the future and moving back with the past. The difference between stretching your arms up and addressing the cosmos is profound. One is about using bones and muscles, the other is about communing with space. The press wrote of Mary Wigman's dances as prayers, they carried something more than the other *Einseltänzerinnen* (female solo dancers). Space, as she used it, became a metaphor for the divine, as she experienced it with Laban.

In a sense Laban had cracked the conundrum 'how do we embody the spiritual in dance?' For him we do it by engaging with the space. It is impossible on this page to demonstrate why he came to that conclusion. For that you need one-to-one contact. What can be said is that that discovery had enormous impact on his theatre work for from it he developed his 'swings' as they were called that became his choreutic scales and rings, templates on the grids, which formed one of the bases of his dance technique and choreographic vocabulary. The other basis was his eukinetic principles of rhythm, dynamics and phrasing. From these studies he knew how to create all manner of movement pattern variations, how to colour them with all manner of dynamic expressivity, harmonic patterns, grotesque patterns and so forth. The Monte Verita experiments over two long summers formed the very stuff from which his dance theatre work from 1919 to 1936 was made. It enabled him to discover how to make movement meaningful, and so how to embody in dance his ideas and

---

25 Later Laban used the word 'scaffold' instead of grid, like a scaffolding outside a building, with movement twining in and through, round and over it. *Choreutics*, 1966.

cultural concerns from his youth, from Paris and from Munich.[26]

The first performances of the *Tanz-Ton-Wort* school in Munich, held in the Museum's performance space, on dance without music, with Karl Weysel and Marie Wiegmann leading an ensemble, were received with surprise and enthusiasm. Wiegmann was immediately recognised as 'a phenomenal talent'. The programme of solos, duos, a trio and a few group pieces were all with non-literal titles, *Lento IV, Formate, Rhythmic Sequence*. The programme ended with Wiegmann's *Hexentanz*, her Witches Dance. If you have ever seen it you would never forget it. It is an extreme, grotesque piece seated on the floor, a drummer underscoring her bizarre barrage of movement expletives. Her talent, exposing as it did Laban's depth of purpose, his *Les Fauves* in movement, contributed enormously to Laban's reputation and to his work being noticed.

August 1914, the fateful date of the beginning of hostilities of WWI, presented Laban with a dilemma. He was thirty-five years old, of military age and a trained officer. Hungarians were expected to fight for Germany. He decided to stay in neutral Switzerland, moving to Zurich to be joined there by artists from all over Europe fleeing the monstrosity of war. So began what I have named 'The Nightmare Years' in my biography of Laban, when he tried to keep together the impossible, his wife Maja, now with four children, his lover Suzanne Perrottet also pregnant, dancers, and his undiminished quest for knowledge and dance making, with the overriding burden of some how finding means to house them all and finance it all.

German-speaking Switzerland, very conventional by habit, was invaded not only by Laban's *ménage a trois* and small group of followers but by an array of writer/painter/poets led by the Romanian, Tristan Tzara. They opened their Cabaret Voltaire in the centre of the town and commenced to shock, bully, astound and appall in 'Dada' events, in a spirit of fury at where 'reason and causality' had led the world, to the destruction of all that was human.

From Hans Richter's book *Dada: Art and Anti Art* the reader can gain a flavour of the furore in Zurich. Chance and the spontaneous were the means used by the Dadaists as weapons to waylay the unsuspecting public in improvised cacophonies of every sort of performance turned on its head.

I described the confrontation of their ideology with Laban's thus:

> The Dada message (or rather messages for the manifestos proclaimed a series of disorganised non-credos), was nihilistic – a transient, potent protest at the mess the world had got itself into and the impotence of the artist within it. Laban protested too. But instead suggested an alternative way forward, rooted in a free body. Tzara's freeing of it focused on those part usually kept private, anus,

26 See the DVD Living Architecture, directed by Valerie Preston-Dunlop and Anna Carlisle which illustrates the scales and rings. Verve Publishing. 2008.

1.1 Self portrait as a cadet in the
Austro-Hungarian Army, 1893,
signed Rudi.

1.2 Rudolf Laban in his atelier, Boulevard Montparnasse, Paris, 1903-1904.

1.3 Laban's drawing of his design for a theatre for dance.

1.4 Rudolf Laban and his students at Monte Verita 1913. Photographer: Johan Adam Meisenbach.

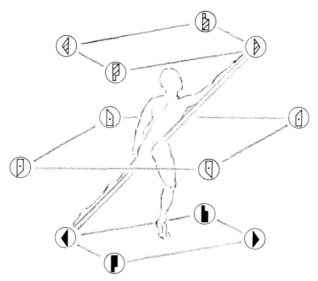

1.5 Drawing of the basic icosahedral grid.

1.6 Rudolf Laban c 1915.

1.7 Green and orange costume design for Marie Wiegmann in *Der Spielmann* (The Fiddler).

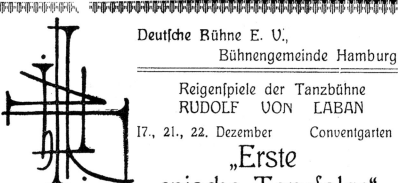

Deutſche Bühne E. V.,
Bühnengemeinde Hamburg

Reigenſpiele der Tanzbühne
RUDOLF VON LABAN

17., 21., 22. Dezember   Conventgarten

„Erste
epische Tanzfolge"

(Die Geblendeten).

Vier Reigen

Begleitende Klangspiele: Am Flügel:
Friedrich Wilckens   **Richard Goldschmied**

Gestaltung der Bühneneinrichtung E. C. Thomassow v. Deutsch. Schauspielhaus

Bechsteinflügel aus der Niederlage Eduard Otto

Beleuchtung Firma Carl Stuhr

1. Reigen:

Auftakt - Einzeltanz: Minne Mampoteng (weiß) -
Schreitende Gruppe und Einzeltanz: Sylvia
Bodmer (silbern) — Zwischenspiel: Minne
Mampoteng und Ingeborg Roon - Schreitende
Gruppe und Dreitanz mit Klangspiel - Gruppen-
Raumspiel - Tanz mit Klangspiel: Dussia Bereska
(weiß) Überleitung - Gruppengebärde.

2. Reigen:

Vorspiel - Tanz: Ingeborg Roon - Männlicher
Tanz: Jens Keiths - Schreitende Gruppe und
Einzeltanz: Gertrud Löser (blau) - Gruppenspiel
von vier Paaren - Einzeltanz Edgar Frank -
Gruppenbewegung - Einzeltanz mit Gruppen-
Begleitung: Claire Ther¡al (weißrot) - Schreite-
tanz zu Dreien.

P A U S E

1.8 Theatre programme for *Erste Epische Tanzfolge*, 1922.

3. *Reigen*:

Grotesker Zweitanz: Troplowitz, Roon - Gruppen=
spiel in dunklen Schleiern mit Klangspiel -
Einzeltanz mit Klangspiel: Sylvia Bodmer (silbern)
- Überleitung - Männlicher Gruppentanz mit
Klangspiel - Gruppenbewegung - Einzeltanz:
Khaven Joos (dunkelgrün).

4. *Reigen*:

Gruppenreigen in dunklen Schleiern - Einmarsch -
Männertanz mit Klangspiel • Einzeltanz: Mario
Volcard (rot) - Gruppenbewegung mit Klangspiel -
Überleitung - Weiblicher Einzeltanz mit männ-
licher Gruppenbegleitung: Dussia Bereska -
Aufzug - Abschließende Gruppengebärde.

Die Tanzfolge wurde früher „Die Geblendeten" genannt,
da in ihr die Blendung durch das vielfache Gefüge der Gewalten und Leidenschaften tänzerisch dargestellt wird.

Mitwirkende:
Vortänzer: Dussia Bereska

Bereska (weiß), Bodmer (silbern), Joos (dunkelgrün), Löser (blau),
Volcard (rot), Mampoteng, Roon (weiß), Frank, Keiths (golden),
Troplowitz (grün-schwarz), Therwal (rosa), Feist, Mené, Müller,
Neggo, Schek (in lila Schleiern), Die Trommler: Knust, Wedekind.

Wiederholungen von „Erste epische Tanzfolge"
21. und 22. Dezember, 7½ Uhr, Conventgarten

„Der schwingende Tempel" 18., 19. und 20. Dezember
CONVENTGARTEN

Für Inhaber der Reihenkarten zum 14., 17. und 20. Dezember weisen wir
darauf hin, daß am 17. (Sonntag-vorm.) die „1. Epische Tanzfolge" und am
20. Dezember „Der schwingende Tempel" aufgeführt werden.

Karten zu allen Veranstaltungen sind zu haben
Deutsche Bühne, Holsenplatz 1, in den bekannten Vorverkaufsstellen und an
den Abendkassen

Die 1. Jahresausgabe der Deutschen Bühne E. V. (Unsere Theaterkultur-
Bestrebungen) liegt am Eingang des Saales aus. Preis M. 100,—
(im Buchhandel etwa M. 400,—)

1.8 continued

1.9 *Gaukelei* (Illusions) 1923. Photographer R. Schellenberg.

1.10 Laban's drawing of The Tyrant in *Gaukelei*.

1.11 Men's group of the Hamburg Movement Choir.

1.12 Publicity material for Gert Ruth Loeszer and Rudolf Laban tour on characters in Wagner operas, 1925.

Aus den Programmen:

TRISTAN UND ISOLDE

KLINGSOR UND KUNDRY

BACCHANAL

und andere Tänze
Musik von Richard Wagner

STUMME TÄNZE

Burlesken
Satiren
Grotesken

RUDOLF VON LABAN
GERT RUTH LOESZER

Die neuen Presseauszüge!

1.13 One of the Wagner Duos. Rudolf Laban and
Gertrud Loeszer, 1925.

1.14 Drawing by Laban of *Narrenspiegel* (The Fool's Mirror).

1.15 Poster advertising a performance of *Don Juan* and *Narrenspiegel* 1926.

1.16 Rudolf Laban, in the programme for *Don Juan* and *Narrenspiegel* 1926.

1.17 *Don Juan*. Rudolf Laban, Dussia Bereska and Herman Robst with dancers from Hertha Feist's movement choir, 1926.

1.18 Dussia Bereska, director of the Kammertanzbühne Laban/ Bereska, 1928.

1.19 Rudolf Laban with the soloists of the State Opera Berlin, 1930.

1.20 *Vom Tauwind und der Neuen Freude*, 1936, Dietrich Eckart open air theatre, Berlin.

penis, vagina, nipple, armpit. Laban's method removed the corsets, tore down the decorous social façade and encouraged a flowering of the public parts, the torso, shoulders, legs, hips, in expression.[27]

While Laban attended the Cabaret 'with his ladies' it was his dancers Mary Wiegmann, Maria Vanselow, Sophie Taüber, Suzanne Perrottet, Maja Kruscel, Käthe Wulff and others, many of them artists in their own right, who participated, emotionally and practically. As Richter emphasised., 'chance became our trademark'. At the Cabaret chance created poetry, song, story, performance, incomprehensible, chaotic, exploratory, where for Laban chance was the very stuff of improvisation in dance through which he discovered the hidden order in movement. **1.6**

Richter comments on 'Laban's revolutionary contribution to choreography' so presumably that revolutionary quality must have been displayed in the only work he made in Zurich, *Der Spielmann* (The Fiddler). The fairy story behind it, related in his autobiography, sounds far removed from revolution or radical chance. But the way he treated it offered a counter radicalism to that confounding the visitors to the Cabaret Voltaire. **1.7**

He returned to Monte Verita for one quite extraordinary event in summer 1917 – a Rosicrucian festival of nature, *The Song to the Sun*. The setting was on the Ascona hillside, sheltered on three sides by clumps of trees and on the fourth side a descending hill to Lake Maggiore. The event centred on a fireplace of boulders where dancers gathered, spread, surrounded, addressed the earth and the dimming sky until a speaker emerged up the hill timed exactly to coincide with the setting sun over the lake. As he declaimed his poem the bonfire lit and was fanned by dancing children and women from the spectators. A final poem to the twilight was said surrounded by a solemn dance that became a procession leading the public out of the meadow. That was part one. Part two began at midnight and was a witches Sabbath with bonfires, leaping dancers masked with twigs and grass, played on the peak of the hill with bizarre rocks overlooking meadows lit by flaming lanterns. Part three commenced at dawn on an east-facing meadow.

> On the horizon the disc of the rising sun appeared and glowed through the dancers' garments. Wave upon wave of joyful dancers...[28]

saluted the dawning day in a celebration of renewal. This was no theatre work but I include it since it underlies the bizarre, near madness, of the mood during the years of the bestial and catastrophic war and the extremes to which Laban was prepared to go. This was a *Les Fauves* celebration.

Laban spent the Zurich years in constant stress, desperately trying to find sponsorship for his quest, working all hours by teaching, lecturing on

---

27 Preston-Dunlop, V. 1998, p.45.

28 Laban 1935, pp 158 – 60.

cultural history, preparing the text for *Die Welt des Tänzers* (The Dancer's World), dodging the Hungarian military, dodging the Swiss immigration who wanted to throw him out because he had no money, appointed Grand Master of the Zurich Rosicrucian lodge, his complex family life, his bipolar state of mind. From a dance theatre perspective these years were barren but they did nothing to lessen his will to continue and for sure he carried with him something of the Dada explosion when he began his main dance theatre career in 1919.

Stuttgart, Mannheim and Hamburg

When the war ended, Laban, in a state of near physical and financial collapse, eventually gained immigration permission to stay in Germany.[29] He came to an amicable agreement with Maja Lederer, with their five children, and Suzanne Perrottet with her son, that he was not capable of combining the responsibilities of parenthood with his quest. Lederer returned to Munich and Perrottet remained in Zurich.

Dussia Bereska, with his group since 1916, went before him to Stuttgart where his fame enabled him to gather a group around him almost immediately. He started training them in his methods and looked for an opportunity to demonstrate their work. The opportunity came for a guest season at Mannheim National Theatre in December 1921 to choreograph for the opera. But he found it impossible to work with the resident ballet troupe. He asked for creativity, they demanded he teach them the steps. He needed them to work as an egalitarian ensemble, they pulled rank and demanded that the soloists had a special celebrity slot. In the end his own unpolished but collaborative dancers took over. The opera was Wagner's *Tannhaüser* with its celebrated *Bacchanal*. It was received with dismay by the tradition-loving opera buffs but as decidedly intriguing by others.

They also performed a first draft of *Die Geblendeten* (The Deluded), Laban's social critique of celebrity culture. It was reworked for the first performances in Hamburg in December 1922 renamed *Erste Epische Tanzfolge* (First Epic Dance Sequence).**1.8** These are discussed in the chapter on recreating *Der Schwingende Tempel*. They were successful enough for the Württemberg State Theatre in Stuttgart to offer him a permanent residency. There his group performed *Oben und Unten* (Above and Below) also titled *Himmel und Erde* (Heaven and Earth) and toured it successfully over the next months. It was an amusing and interestingly staged piece with the performance space divided on two levels, where the moon, evening star and comets have their domain 'above' and get entangled with the 'stargazers' and their entourage

29 Through the Treaty of Versaille The Austro Hungarian empire was split up. Bratislava became part of Czechoslovakia but Laban had Hungarian nationality and no automatic residency in Germany.

on earth below. The piece remained in the Kammertanz repertory and is discussed further in that chapter.

From these experiences he decided that to make work in the way he envisioned he would have to form his own company, a daunting thought with its financial and logistic challenges. This he set out to do with an enlarged and exceptional group of inspired men and women prepared to dance and live as a sharing commune who became the *Tanzbühne Laban* (Laban's Dance Theatre). These people were not your usual ballet trained youngsters. Several of the men had survived trench warfare. Albrecht Knust a folk dancer before the war, was severely shell shocked. The women were an international group, leaving behind ballet in their own countries. How they prepared over the next month in rural Gleschendorf is vividly described in Laban's autobiography:

> There we [took[up our quarters and split into groups with three or four or even more to a house. We could not find a covered hall for our rehearsals anywhere in the neighbourhood so instead we used a big meadow near a lake... Then it began to rain and rain for weeks and months. We practised in small groups of five to seven in the halls of nearby village inns.[30]

In these circumstances *Der Schwingende Tempel* was rehearsed.

At their first appearance as a company in December 1922, in Hamburg. *Tanzbühne Laban* performed a completed *Die Geblendeten, Fausts Erlösung* (Faust's Release) and *Der Schwingende Tempel* (The Swinging Temple). These three works are discussed in the chapter on the recreation of *The Swinging Temple.*

His next major endeavour, a 'dance-ballad, was *Gaukelei* (Illusions), his most well known choreography, premiered in 1923. **1.9, 1.10,** It is a social critique of the rise and fall of a tyrannical character commented on by the jester (*Gaukler*). It proved to be a powerful piece of political theatre at a time when potential leaders from the far right and the far left were battling it out in the German streets as the Weimar Republic tried to find a political solution to postwar chaos. The main characters were a jester, the tyrant (played by Laban), a beggar, a hangman, a juggler, a princess, and ensemble. Laban organised it as an interplay of archetypes, giving the spectator moments of compassion for the poor, anxiety for the innocent, fear of death, admiration-cum-pity for the delusion of power, amusement by joking capers.[31]

Laban had a conviction about the responsibility of the artist for his audience:

These many people are not just customers and buyers, nor are we artists just

30 Laban, 1935, p. 99.

31 *Gaukelei* was recreated by Kurt Jooss in 1930 for his company in Essen and by Aurel Milloss with the Dusseldorf opera ballet in 1935, a brave and risky choice with the Nazi authorities vetting every performance.

egocentric producers who are allowed to dream our dreams in isolation. We are all one, and what is at stake is the universal soul out of which and for which we have to create.[32]

Whatever plans Laban had for his company after *Gaukelei* were almost immediately thwarted by the collapse of Germany's currency. The terrifying 1000% inflation meant the value of any money they had earned diminished into nothing. To cope his community made and toured small *Kammertanz* works (Chamber Dances). The *Tanzbühne* made one international tour in June 1924 and the disastrous outcome is discussed in the chapter on the recreation of the Kammertanz solos and duos.[33]

The variety of Laban's choreographic opportunities in Hamburg was evident. In May 1923 he presented his version of the popular Richard Strauss score *Josephslegende* (Joseph's story) at the Hamburg City Theatre, the premiere having been given by the Diaghilev Ballets Russes. He rarely worked with an existing score unless it was written specifically for dance, which this score was. Being the biblical story of Potiphar's wife and Joseph it offered Dussia Bereska a leading role. Laban went on in the same year to choreograph incidental dances at the City Theatre for Shakespeare's *Winter's Tale* and *A Midsummer Night's Dream* using his own company.

Later in the year in quite another genre his first major group work for Hamburg's amateur movement choir was performed, *Lichtwende* (Dawning Light). The essential differences between a movement choir work and a theatre work is that the former is primarily made for the participants, to enhance the sense of community and belonging, a topic close to Laban's heart. He wrote that a community based on 'mutuality' and promoting the development of each individual in the group is essential to the wellbeing of a culture.[34] This was to cause his dismissal in 1936 being in direct conflict with the National Socialist's concept of community as people en masse conforming to political dogma.

Later movement choir works included *Agamemnons Tod* (Death of Agamemnon), *Dämmernden Rhythmen* (Dawning Rhythms), *Alltag und Fest* (Everyday and Festive Days). Notable was the men's group of the Hamburg Movement Choir, where he put into practice his conviction that if dance was to be taken seriously as an art form it must be represented by men as well as women. **1.11**

Despite the financial difficulties Laban continued to choreograph for his

---

32 Laban, 1935, p.94.

33 Evelyn Dörr's Appendix in her 2008 text lists the names of the copious number of small works made in the 1920s which include pure movement pieces, *Formate, Ikosaeder, Rhythmische Suite*, to comedies *Interpunktionestanz* and *Klub der Sonderlinge* and grotesque dances *Das Grauen (Horror)* and *Kampf (Battle.)*

34 Laban, 1935, p 84

Tanzbühne. He was likened by his circle to a volcano. An outpouring of ever emerging creative ideas seemed to tumble out of him. His choreographies were one strand of this creativity. He never intended they should lose their immediacy and become fixed for he was already turning his mind to the next as he completed the one in rehearsal, in fact on many occasions leaving an assistant to complete the process.

In spring 1925 he and Gertrud Loeszer set out on a tour with what can only be described as an audacious series of duos on the leading characters in Wagner's Ring Cycle, Tristan and Isolde, Klingsor and Kindry from *Parsifal*, Alberich and Mimne from *Das Rheingold*. But they were danced without music. **1.12, 1.13** The spirit of experiment was evident. Can this be done successfully was his question? Their second programme entitled *Choreographische Tanz-Composition* was composed of dances written in notation, in this case the so-called swallowtail notation, his interim method, for the final solutions for the system were not published until summer 1928. The public saw both, the dance and its score.

Terpsichore, *Narrenspiegel* (The Fool's Mirror) and *Don Juan* were full evening's works that the *Tanzbühne Laban* toured widely in 1925 and 26, Laban performing in all of them. A dance drama, *Terpsichore*, was a working of Handel's opera for singers and dancers, Terpsichore being the muse of dance. The characters are Terpsichore, a dancer, in this case Bereska, Apollo a soprano, Erato a contralto or counter tenor, Graces, a Youth, and a Faun, all dancers. *Terpsichore* is a baroque composition with dances interspersed between solos and duet singing.

Narrenspiegel was a play on the inseparability of opposites, Joy/Grief, Pride/Humility, Love/Hate.

> It was the most successful of my dance plays – at least the one I performed most often... In the Fool's Mirror there were two Reigen or, if you prefer it, two acts, one of which could be called the dance of life and the other the dance of death.

The same characters appeared in both acts reflecting their duality. Pride/Humility was a solemn gentleman, Joy/Grief an emotional woman, and Love/Hate a woman who loved life and hated death. It reflected Laban's own emotional states of exhileration when things went well followed by profound depression and personal doubt.**1.14, 1.15**

For *Don Juan* he experimented by including movement choir members as the supporting group, on a par with a *corps de ballet*. In each city that they played he employed the movement choir of that city. It was remarkable that by 1925/6 trained *Bewegungschor Laban* flourished in so many cities. It was in performing the last gruesome scene in which Don Juan 'is torn to pieces by the spirits of hell' that the movement choir members were fatally ill-prepared. He should disappear in a cloud of flame to land on a strategically placed mattress but instead he landed on the hard floor and

Laban concentrated on ways in which his vision for dance as a respected independent art form could be promoted. He had published three books in 1926, *Choreographie, Gymnastik und Tanz* (Exercise and Dance) and *Des Kindes Gymnastik und Tanz* (Exercise and Dance for Children) He opened his *Choreographisches Institut* in Würzberg the same year, his research institute, with which he hoped to collaborate with both theatre people and university people on the pressing issues for dance development. It moved to Berlin Grunenwald a year later. This was indeed the first institute for practical scholarship, for the artist as researcher. Run by an experienced faculty it attracted able students, people already on the ladder of a career in dance such as the classically trained Aurel Milloss who went on to combine ballet with the New Dance in his conspicuous career as a choreographer.

Laban planned a government- or state-supported dance high school to safeguard the innovations that he had instituted, the progress that had undoubtedly been made in the previous decades and the work that was now being undertaken by his erstwhile pupils, and those of Mary Wigman. The German Dance had definitely arrived and needed establishment recognition.[39] But its realisation was delayed until 1935 and then, tragically and ideologically too late.

1928 saw the second Dancers' Congress held at Essen, directed by Kurt Jooss, where Laban concentrated on presenting the completed notation. Alfred Schlee, an editor from Universal Edition, followed this up by publishing an academic journal *Schrifttanz*, the first of its kind, on dance writing of all sorts including the notation. It ran with editions four times a year from 1928 until 1932 when the third financial crisis in Germany caused its closure. For the performances at the Essen Congress Bereska directed the *Kammertanz Laban* presentation of *Die Grünen Clowns* (Green Clowns). Its recreations in 1987 and 2008 are discussed in the chapter of that name.

During the 1928/29 season Bereska took the *Kammertanzbühne Laban-Bereska* on extensive tours. The archive details eighty performances across Germany usually in the town theatre, occasionally the opera house, with short tours to Lithuania, Poland, Holland, Paris, Rome, Jugoslavia, Prague, Graz and Switzerland. The accounts show that they earned well and the tour report details their reception as 'mostly good or very good, occasionally sold out despite a bad review.'

Berlin

In the aftermath of the Wall Street crash of 1929 all postwar American investment in Germany collapsed making thousands of workers redundant.

---

39 Maletic, Vera in McCaw, D. *The Laban Source book*, London Routledge 2011. Maletic discusses the purpose of the *Choreographishes Institut* and Laban's lecture presentations at the First Dancers' Congress.

Unemployment soared. Touring had to stop. Keeping the *Institut* as an independent organisation became impossible so it was absorbed into the Central Laban School now at Essen under the direction of Kurt Jooss. The political situation worsened with National Socialism gaining ground. In this uncertainty Laban was appointed to the top post in German dance, Director of Movement to the Prussian State Theatres, centred on the famous Opera House at Unter den Linden, Berlin. He moved to Berlin in summer 1930 and became a full-time employee for the first time in his life.

As part of his remit he was responsible for the dances in the summer season at the internationally renowned Bayreuth Opera, led by the anti-semitic Wagner family and frequented by Adolf Hitler. Dussia Bereska, being Jewish, left Germany to open a Laban school in Paris, Gertrud Snell going to teach with her. At Bayreuth Laban, assisted by Jooss, choreographed the Bacchanal, reviewed as a sensation, 'flaming, surging, wild, entwined' for Wagner's *Tannhaüser*. Laban admired Wagner:

> To me Wagner was not only a renewer and prophet of the arts of poetry and music. Since both through his writings and from the mouths of his personal collaborators I had the good fortune to get to know his tremendous way of thinking in terms of movement. I can say that he was also a decisive influence on the art of movement.[40]

Laban started a four-year period of choreographing incidental dances for opera. Some critics doubted whether his aesthetic would sit well with the Berlin opera audiences but his first assignment, the Polovtsian Dances in Borodin's *Prince Igor*, were received with acclaim, not only for the new choreography itself but because the critics judged the occasion to augur well for the future of German dance. His next noticed choreography was the Dance of the Seven Veils in Strauss's dark opera *Salome*. So far so good, but he rapidly fell out with the soloists of the ballet, a repetition of his issues at the National Theatre in Mannheim. **1.19** Giving the soloists the option to work as an ensemble with the corps de ballet or leave, they left, loudly and publicly, as reported in the *Sozialistischen Monatshefte* dated May 1931. With an ensemble and his wide knowledge of national and social dance material he choreographed often insignificant incidental dances for Wagner's *Meistersingers*, Charpentier's *Louise*, Strauss' *A Night in Venice*, Bizet's *Carmen*, Verdi's *La Traviata* and *Sicilian Vespers*, Wagner's *Rienzi* and so on. An additional unique feature of his appointment was the inclusion of Susanne Ivers as notator. Three of her scores still exist.

It is not surprising that he had some difficulty with the annual *Tanzabend* (Evening of Dance) His preferred way of working was with creative dancers and a rehearsal director, Bereska. In Berlin he had neither. He did give one interpretation of Debussy's *Jeux* the scenario of which was a triangle of

40 Laban 1935, p.174.

tension and release between two women and one man engaged in a game of tennis, first choreographed by Nijinsky.

Progress was confounded by Germany's third financial crisis in 1932. All budgets at the opera were slashed. Mid-way through Laban's opera contract Adolf Hitler became head of state and tightened the Nazi domination of culture. The archives of the Berlin Opera show how the racial laws impacted on everyone, and these edicts landed on Laban's desk. He and everyone employed by the *Reichskulturkammer* (State Chamber of Culture) had to prove their Aryan background including the children in the opera's ballet school.

His last dance theatre work, after another *Tannhaüser*, Reznicek's *Donna Diana* and Bizet's *Pearlfishers* was, incongruously, a reworking of a traditional ballet *Dornröschen* (Sleeping Beauty). The double irony was that, on completion of his contract, his role at the Opera House was passed to Lizzie Maudrik, a traditional ballet mistress. For a matinée before his Sleeping Beauty she put on *Puppenfee* (the Fairy Doll). The influence of New Dance at the opera house was well and truly over.

From 1934 he was appointed Director of the *Deutsche Tanzbühne*, (German Dance Theatre) the politically dominated organisation, overseeing dance throughout Germany, under Joseph Goebbels, Minister of Propaganda. Before long a department was created for him titled the Master Academy for Dance which seemed to be the fulfillment of his dreams of establishing a state sponsored training facility for dancers with library, notation and archive. Evelyn Dörr traces the tightrope that he walked to try to balance his dream with the reality of the Nazi stranglehold on culture.[41]

1935 saw the preparations for what has been dubbed Hitler's Games, the Olympics held in Berlin in the summer of 1936 designed as an accolade to Nazi Germany. Laban was responsible for much of the cultural programme alongside the sport. Gertrud Snell returned from Paris to work as his assistant in running the fraught International Choreographic Competition of 1935 for which Hitler demanded that a German company must win, and his last work in Germany *Vom Tauwind und der neuen Freude* (The Spring Wind and the New Joy). It was not a theatre work so has no rightful place in this text but it was so significant for the man that I cannot omit it. Laban's autobiography *Ein Leben für den Tanz* (A Life for Dance) was published that year, with his fundament belief in the value of the individual and dance for all clearly stated, in direct conflict with the national dogma of discrimination and conformity. **1.20**

In one of my interviews with Snell she divulged that they were always nervous that the performance would be disallowed. *Tauwind* was the largest

---

41 Dörr, E. *Rudolf Laban: the Dancer of the Crystal*. Plymouth: Scarecrow Press. 2008, pp.160-169.

movement choir piece ever attempted, over one thousand dancers, with choirs from all over Germany participating. With Albrecht Knust's help the choreography was notated and sent to the participating choirs who rehearsed from it. The two people I interviewed years later who saw the closed dress rehearsal, watched and vetted by both Goebbels and Hitler, said:

> One has rarely seen such dedication, such inner fire, such achievement from lay performers in the other arts – and most importantly the spark of enthusiasm did not remain confined to the stage but rather spread to everyone present.[42]

But Goebbels disagreed. He wrote in his diary:

> It is dressed in our clothes but has nothing to do with us.

And he forbade its performance. Laban was dismissed and fled Germany in 1937 arriving in Great Britain in 1938, a destitute refugee. He never made dance theatre works again.

The Nazi machine obliterated Laban from German culture, forbidding his books, his notation, turning his schools into *Kraft durch Freude* (Strength through Joy) training centres.

The last twenty years of his life in England were productive nevertheless, but their scope was limited by his status as an enemy alien when World War II began in 1939. As soon as he recovered his health sufficiently he gained employment in industry promoting ways in which the repetitive dehumanising work of the production line might be improved. He expanded his theory of eukinetics into a theory of human effort in work, soon expanded into the realm of management looking at how efficient human interaction is influenced by the dynamics of the behaviour of those in charge. It became the sophisticated study known today as Effort.[43] As soon as permitted after the war he developed expressive effort with actors at Bradford Civic Theatre and Joan Littlewood's Theatre Workshop, and with mentally ill patients at Withymead psychotherapy centre. [44] This set off new training methods in drama schools and kick started the profession of Dance Movement Therapy in the United Kingdom.

His involvement with dance took the form of promoting creative movement and dance for all, with his assistant Lisa Ullmann, taken up rapidly by the British government and introduced for boys and girls as Modern Educational Dance in the school education system.[45] Together they opened The Art of Movement Studio that developed over the years from a struggling post-war studio in Manchester to the renowned dance department of Trinity Laban

---

42 Yat Malmgren, Swedish actor studying with Wigman, Helen Priest Rogers, American studying notation with Knust. Interviews. Laban Collection.

43 Laban, R. *Effort*. London: Macdonald & Evans. 1947.

44 Laban, R. *Mastery of Movement*. London: Macdonald & Evans. 1950.

45 Laban, R. *Modern Educational Dance*. London: Macdonald & Evans 1948.

Conservatoire for Music and Dance in London that it is today.

Laban died in 1958, his Labanotation established in New York at the Dance Notation Bureau and as Kinetography Laban in continental Europe. His effort theory became known in the USA as Laban Movement Analysis. It was not until some years after his death that Laban-based Choreological Studies was established for the training of professional dancers in England, and taken abroad through specialist courses for established practitioners. It has taken until now to present his pioneering theatre works so that today's performing arts world can see for themselves where it all began, in Germany in the 1920s.

Chapter Two
Archival resources for practical historiography and re-creation

Archival records of Rudolf Laban's theatre work are scattered. He left Germany in 1937 under difficult circumstances and had to leave his personal archive with his friend Marie-Luise Lieschke for safe keeping in her house in Plauen. Immediately after World War II Plauen was in the Russian section of Germany so once 'the iron curtain', as Winston Churchill named it, came down, closing the east from the west, recovering the archives became impossible and contact was lost. Later John Hodgson, professor from Bretton Hall College, managed to get through and locate the house and was able to retrieve some materials. His collection is housed in the Brotherton Library of Leeds University. The Tanzarchiv in Leipzig[1] recovered the remainder which is maintained as a collection in their large holding of German dance particularly of the inter-war years and Dance in the GDR.

The archives of Laban's British period (1938-58) are held at the National Resource Centre for Dance at Surrey University in Guildford but Laban was not undertaking theatre work at that time. He concentrated on what was permitted to him as an alien during the war years, namely movement study in industry, and postwar, on creative dance for children and adults, movement for actors and in therapy and what has become known as movement profiling. This holding includes a small amount on Laban's dance theatre work collected by his associate Lisa Ullmann.

Trinity Laban Conservatoire of Music and Dance in London hold the Laban Collection, the core of which is a large group of paper and electronic materials that I gathered as a postdoctoral research project in the latter 1980s. I searched for evidence in the cities of Germany, France, Switzerland, Italy and Austria where Laban had worked and toured between 1900 and 1936. The newspaper archives, the opera house archives, the city archives, Bauhaus and Dada archives, antiquarian book and journal collections, university library collections all revealed evidence of a vibrant dance culture that, by nature of its essential ephemerality and sparse photographic record, had become all but lost. It was certainly ignored by cultural historians, of whom John Willet is an example,[2] who only included passing reference to Laban's pupil Mary Wigman and to the *korperkultur* or body culture groups, many with images of nudity.

The 1999 scholarly doctoral thesis of Evelyn Dörr on *Rudolf von Laban: Leben und Werk des Kunstlers 1879-1936* draws from the Leipzig Tanzarchiv

---

1 *Tanzarchiv* collections are now held by Leipzig University.
2 Willett, J. *The New Sobriety, 1917-33*. London: Thames and Hudson. 1978.

and newspaper collections and is a detailed record of what went on from the perspective of published documents. Her later book draws on letters that give insight into the personal traumas of life.[3] Dörr does not attempt to get at the choreographic processes or the insider view of what it was like to be working with Laban.[4] For that another approach is necessary. Her book includes an appendix listing Laban's dances by premiere which can give a skewed idea of what was a significant event and what was not. Unfortunately her translator gives English titles to the choreographic works some of which are bizarre and misleading.

Practical historiography is one of the studies that Trinity Laban Conservatoire of Music and Dance specialises in. For example, the dancers study Martha Graham by not only having Graham technique classes but by performing remountings of her repertoire directed by people who have been through the company or school.[5] They study Cunningham Technique and perform a Merce Cunningham work directed by someone from the Cunningham stable.[6] They study Rudolf Laban through Laban-based technique, dancing his movement scales and rings and through recreating his works directed by people with first-hand knowledge of his methods.[7]

To achieve that level of work you need practitioners steeped in the techniques as well as archival resources of the works as products plus an understanding of the choreographic methods by which they were made. You need scholars who are both researchers and dancers. Remounting a work depends entirely on the nature of the work and how it was created. In the case of a Graham work rehearsal focuses on matching a performance to an original because Graham's works were completed works, filmed and some notated. The style has a particular intention, movement vocabulary and particular look. A Graham work defies its ephemerality by becoming an iconic repeatable form through intense rehearsal. To remount such a work is a painstaking and deeply scholarly event.

By contrast a Laban work has no iconic surface because his way of working embraced ephemerality. His works were never rehearsed with the aim of creating a reproducible product, their form changed according to circumstance and opportunity, being creative and improvisational

3 Dörr, E. *Rudolf Laban: The Dancer of the Crystal*. Plymouth: The Scarecrow Press. 2008
4 Dörr's *Annotated List of Laban's Works*, while it is a useful chronology, is occasionally seriously misleading as it is on *Der Schwingende Tempel* where she gives a red dancer and a belly dancer as its only 'protagonists'. There is also a question over *Der Schwingende Gewalten* where under that title she has an evening of varied dances from the Kammertanz repertoire, the programme for 1924 in the Laban Collection shows a touring version of *Der Schwingende Tempel*.
5 *Diversion of Angels, Primitive Mysteries*.
6 *Scramble*.
7 *Die Grünen Clowns* 2008, 2009, *Nacht* 2010, 2011, *Der Schwingende Tempel* 2012.

in performance.[8] However, the core of a Laban work remains in each instantiation, lying in the tasks given to the dancers and his method of editing and directing what they produce.

Engaging with dance works that have not been filmed or notated and are apparently lost leads one to archeochoreological methods. Archaeology is defined as 'the technique of studying man's past using material remains as a primary source,'[9] so the problem for the dance archaeologist is to sort out what 'material remains' might consist in for a work. There the dancer as living archive takes on a special role. If you are remounting a work from a score or from a film the living body memory of people trained in the style or who danced in the work is required to locate the authenticity of the work. If you are recreating a work from the archival traces, as we are with Laban's works, the body memory becomes especially significant.

As part of the Laban Collection project, undertaken in the 1980s, and the most essential for re-finding his work, I focused on locating any members of his *Tanzbühne* companies who might still be living from whom I might learn his choreographic practice.

Fritz Klingenbeck was the first person I located. A retired theatre Intendant in Vienna he had been part of the close circle around Laban at the time when Laban was wrestling to complete his dance notation. He was able to tell me of his experiences as a dancer in *Nacht* and as a notation assistant between 1925 and 1929 and he provided photographs of the rehearsals for the premiere of *Der Schwingende Tempel* in 1922.

Käthe Wulff, at almost a hundred years old, was still teaching in her Basel studio. A collaborator with Laban from 1913 she gave me insight into Laban's dance activity on Monte Verita and his views on the iconoclastic Dada group's 'events' at their Café Voltaire in Zurich during WWI, she being a participant, and Laban an audience member. Wulff danced in his early piece *Der Spielmann (The Fiddler)*, produced in Zurich in 1917. *Die Klub der Sonderlingen* (The Club of the Eccentrics), part of the suite *Die Grünen Clowns*, echoes the Dadaists' focus on the bizarre. Wulff gave me an improvisation class based on Laban's early ideas on the body, space and dynamics. Having been a student of Laban's myself from 1947 I knew the material in its more sophisticated form developed by Laban in those thirty intervening years. The experience with Wulff showed me where his ideas on movement were at the beginning of his productive choreographic period.

8 *Der Schwingende Tempel* appeared first in 1922 as a full evening ensemble work, in 1924 entitled *Der Schwingende Gewalten* as a series of duos, trios, quintets, and in 1952 as an ensemble piece for amateurs titled *The Swinging Cathedral. Die Grünen Clowns*, a suite, appears first as separate pieces, as a suite in December 1927 and a suite of different content in June 1928 at the 2nd Dancers' Congress.

9 *Fontana Dictionary of Modern Thought*, 2nd ed,. eds. Alan Bullock, Oliver Stallbrass, and Stephen Tromley (London: Fontana Press, 1988).

I located **Gertrud Snell** in a retirement home in Hanover. A fount of information and with astounding memory, she had been in Laban's close circle from 1924-29 and 1933-36. A member of the *Kammertanz* group in Hamburg she had performed the solos *Krystall* and *Ikosaheder* being a specialist in Laban's space harmony material. She had danced in *Nacht* and had seen *Die Grünen Clowns*. She had regularly taught notation and space studies. As Laban's secretary and right-hand woman during the Nazi period she had been intimately connected with the creation and politicisation of the huge movement choir work for the 1936 Olympics that caused his downfall, *Tauwind und der neuen Freude*. It was from Snell that I realised how the movement principles embedded in Laban's notation were a crucial ingredient of his creative process as were his spatial scales and rings.

Ilse Loesch I visited in East Berlin. Primarily a leader of community dance and a strongly socialist woman she had started her career as a member of one of Laban's movement choir groups. She had performed in *Ritterballett* in 1927 and had seen the performance of *Nacht* and witnessed its hostile reception while agreeing with the dancers that it was one of Laban's strongest statements on the dark side of Weimar culture.

Aurel Milloss, renowned Hungarian choreographer, I interviewed in Rome. His first acquaintance as a young ballet dancer with Laban was seeing him perform the solos *Marotte* and *Mondäne* at Konstanz. This made such an impression on him that he enrolled in Laban's Choreographisches Institut, when it opened in Berlin in 1927. He was able to tell me of its practical curriculum and research-as-practice culture. In 1935, as choreographer at the Dusseldorf Opera, Milloss had mounted his own version of Laban's 1923 social critique *Gaukelei*. Although critical of some of Laban's work under the Nazis, Milloss was deeply impressed by Laban's audacity in portraying and ridiculing tyrannical leadership in *Gaukelei* and had the courage himself to put the work on in Dusseldorf opera house at a time when flouting Nazi laws on theatre could have cost him his job or worse.

Beatrice Mazzoni had joined Dussia Bereska, Laban's prime soloist and artistic assistant, in her short-lived school in Rome in 1924. The *Tanzbühne* Laban had broken up after being caught by the financial chaos following the now famous inflation of 1923. Penniless in Zagreb they had split, some dancers following Laban back to Hamburg others following Bereska. Mazzoni went on to enroll in Laban's *Choreographisches Institut* at the same time as Milloss. A relative beginner she was an audience member at the performances at the Dancers' Congresses on 1927 and 1928, so witnessed *Ritterballett*, *Nacht* and *Die Grünen Clowns*.

Three crucial collaborators with Laban I already knew well. **Sylvia Bodmer**, performer in *Der Schwingende Tempel* and *Die Geblendeten* in 1921 and '22, had been my composition teacher as a student. I interviewed her in her last years. After a long career as a teacher and director of community dance performances in Frankfurt and later Manchester, her recall of the rehearsals 'in a meadow with thistles' of *Der Schwingende Tempel* in rural Gleschendorf informed me profoundly of Laban's situation, methods and impact. Experienced by Bodmer as life changing, Laban's iconoclastic creativity had seemed to pour from his body as he demanded and received complete absorption and creative commitment from the men and women in his company.

Two fellow dancers with Bodmer in the 1921-22 season were **Kurt Jooss,** a highly talented music student young enough to have missed WWI, and Albrecht Knust, a war-shattered veteran whose first experience of dance had been as a folk dancer. I worked with them both in Germany after WWII where Jooss was director of the dance department of the Folkwanghochshule in Essen and Knust ran its notation studio. Jooss's choreographic ambitions had led him to leave Laban after the 1924 crash and start his own amalgamation of ballet with Laban's labile and dynamic methods. Becoming world famous after winning the International Choreographic Competition in Paris in 1932 with his anti-war ballet *Der Grüne Tisch (The Green Table)* he escaped to England with his Jewish colleagues and his Ballets Jooss in 1934. It was Jooss who engineered Laban's refugee status in 1938 at Dartington Hall in Devon where the philanthropists Dorothy and Leonard Elmhirst had made a haven for artists fleeing the Nazi oppression. Taking part in Jooss's class in Essen in 1952 I could experience and see how his mixing of ballet with choreutics and eukinetics had developed into the Jooss Technique and while touring with the company and witnessing rehearsals of *The Green Table* I could see the effect the ballet discipline had had on Jooss's choice of expressive movement material. The expressionist 'War' section of Laban's *Green Clowns* is a much more corporeal and live-in-the-moment work than the detailed craftsmanship for the soldiers in Jooss's modernist war scene in *The Green Table*.

Albrecht Knust remained with Laban, becoming the key man in the development of the notation and as a movement choir director, until he too was ousted by the Nazis in 1936, managing to lie low in Munich until joining Jooss when the latter returned to Germany after the war. Becoming a short term assistant to Knust I became acutely aware of the details of the notation principles and their choreographic potential as a basic grammar of movement. He had acted as the drummer in *Der Schwingende Tempel*, knew at first hand Laban's approach to the sound of a dance coming out of the movement and never as the starting point for the movement. He had been connected with all Laban's choreographic works, as performer or drummer, rehearsal assistant or notator.

Lisa Ullmann, trained in Laban's methods in Germany. She had come to

England, to Dartington Hall, as a teacher for the Jooss Ballet's school. It was Ullmann who opened the Laban School in Manchester after WWII, where I became a student. Bodmer, married and living in Manchester, worked with her, Laban directing the school's curriculum. Ullmann was not a theatre woman but an exceptional teacher and it was from her that I learned the grammar of movement as choreutic practice, through danced studies on spatial form, and eukinetic practice, through danced studies on dynamic rhythm and Laban's very vigorous 'flying and falling' body training. Bodmer's composition classes brought me centrally into Laban-based compositional method with its strong ingredient of improvisation and the dancer's intention in narrative and especially in abstract material, ensemble sensitivity and precision of non-metric rhythms.

Laban himself gave highly original movement workshops in dance history. When approaching ancient Egyptian dance and the Dervish whirling I now realise that he gave examples from his male duo *Ekstatische* although he never mentioned his own past work by name. I became one of his apprentices and went with him to Pilkington's tile factory where he was employed to achieve higher output. He used his principles of the grammar of movement to harmonise the grossly inorganic repetitive sequences of the workers on the production line. My task was to record in notation each operative's way of working. Notating is simple for full body movement but not, then, for working with machinery nor for small intricate arm and hand moves. Struggling with the notation detail taught me a great deal about movement principles and the subtlety of the rhythm of hand movements such as you find in *Orchidée*. I came to understand Laban's strongly felt attitude to the mechanisation and dehumanisation of industrial workers, a passion that appears in *Die Grünen Clowns, Nacht* and *Der Schwingende Tempel.*

Two people I never met personally were **Dussia Bereska** and Ruth Loeszer, Laban's main performing partners. Bereska was the soloist in *Orchidée*. She appeared in almost all his works often in a leading role. She joined Laban in Zurich in 1916 already a trained dancer. She was probably Russian with a passport name of Olga Feldt. Her talent lay in her dynamic range as a beguiling performer but she soon developed a creative ability to help Laban transform his ideas into works. After WWI when he was establishing himself in Germany, Bereska was essential to him. While he was battling with opera directors, giving lectures on dance culture, writing books, creating a notation, starting a school and researching movement's grammar she pulled together his choreographic sketches, directed the school, took rehearsals and organised tours. She is named as directing *Die Grünen Clowns* in 1928 while he that same morning gave the first public presentation of his notation, a major event in the second Dancers' Congress.

Bereska appears in most of the photographs of rehearsals. She left Germany for Paris in 1929, probably because she was Jewish and Laban's promotion to Berlin as Movement Director (Choreographer) of the Prussian State Theatres took him uncomfortably close to the rising Nazi politics. Laban had great difficulty without her. It confirmed to me that his works were collaborative, part his, part his creative dancers and part his rehearsal director. In the Berlin Opera House at Unter den Linden he was by himself with uncreative ballet dancers and no rehearsal director so no wonder he was not always successful with his opera ballets.

Ruth Loeszer possessed the complementary qualities to Bereska. They were rivals both as dancers and as Laban's lovers. Loeszer was spatial, elegant, an expert performer of his space harmony scales and rings. She alternated with Bereska to dance *Rosetten*. Laban and Loeszer toured a duo season in 1925 with an extraordinary topic, duets on personalities in Wagner operas danced without music, outrageously audacious since Wagner was the icon of German music. Loeszer was rehearsal director for *Die Nacht* but was overall less essential to Laban than Bereska. Being Jewish she was also reluctant to follow him to Berlin.

While working under **Laban**'s direction for four years and staying within his circle for twelve years in all before his death, my body became a living archive of his movement styles and point of view. One fundamental style is organicism, all parts of your body integrating to say the same thing be it dynamic change or a simple phrase of closing and opening. This contrasts with how ballet-trained dancers hold their torso around which their *port de bras* unfold and their legs articulate gestures and steps. Torso involvement is far more exaggerated than in ballet, acute body awareness is trained where surfaces and joints lead the action, lability shifts your weight away from stability. With choreutic awareness the space becomes a virtual partner, embracing it, pushing it, lifting it, penetrating it, leaning on it, scattering it. Dynamic range is huge from intricate sensitive lightness to sweeping powerful strength. Corporeality is a hall mark, Laban dancers do not hide their effort, they share it with the audience and each other, naked skin, flowing hair, bare feet, give the audience dancers that are gendered, social people. The lived sensual experience of moving together is what you share in group collaboration, leading, following, passing, avoiding, touching, confronting. Above all the Laban dancer is creative with improvisation a norm, taking over each other's roles a norm, sound making as well as dancing a norm, dancing in the open where you feel the wind on your body but as well painstakingly rehearsing in the studio.

The personal archive of **Suzanne Perrottet** housed in the *Kunsthaus* in Zurich includes letters between herself and Laban, particularly during their relationship before and during World War I. They give insight into the fundamental first questions that he was asking himself and trying out on Perrottet, a Dalcrose dancer who became his student and assistant for children's dance.

Hans Brandenberg's correspondence with Laban and writings on dramaturgy give an idea of Laban's fascination with the expressivity of movement and forms of theatre and on the primacy of movement as a medium for performance where before him music and spoken language in opera and plays had been the (almost) only modes of theatrical communication.

Mary Wigman, Laban's prime pupil in 1913 and eventual rival, wrote revealingly about Laban as her teacher. All dance archives include material on her copious and widely acclaimed performances. One needs to understand the ways in which she reflects Laban's training and point of view and how she developed her own dance voice and mode of choreography. She was an expressionist phenomenon choreographing around her own central performance as a woman, working at the same time that he functioned as an expressionist artist-researcher working with both men and women and that difference found its way into his experimental modes of theatre making.

Laban's own publication at the time *Die Welt des Tänzers* (The dancer's world), 1920, immediately gives the breadth and radicalism of his thinking. Particular is his notion that the dancer, as the new man of the future,

> strives to interweave clear intellect, deep feeling and strong will into a harmoniously balanced and flexible whole...

in contrast to the received wisdom that these human faculties operate separately and 'brutally'.[10] A recreator of Laban work knows that that is the relationship to have with the dancers. They think-intend-feel as they move and create as people who have something new to say to the world. No wonder Laban had trouble whenever he choreographed with an opera ballet troupe.

His text *Choreographie*, 1926, on the grammar of movement, that was the basis of his pioneering notation system by 1928, provides access to his way of thinking at that time about the principles of movement's spatial form, the polykinetic counterpoint of the body and its dynamic rhythms.

His autobiography *Ein Leben für den Tanz* (A Life for Dance) published in 1935 at a time when he was in great jeopardy in the midst of Nazi Berlin, is his statement of belief, put down to show where he stood and was trying to remain, against all the onslaught of Nazi dogma hitting every artist. Arranged in chapters named after his choreographic works it provides the recreator with an essential reference point as to his thinking on each work, not as a description of the work but as his deeply felt response to the

10 McCaw, D. ed. *The Laban Source Book*. London: Routledge, 2011, chapter The World of the Dancer, p.45.

experiences his culture offered him that led to the work.

With these 'material remains' as a resource, the next stage of recreation can start, the stage of transformation and renewal. Lesley-Anne Sayers puts the essential concepts after working on the Prokofiev, Yakoulov and Massine ballet *Le Pas d'Acier* (The Steel Step) 1927:

> The challenge to researchers afforded by reconstruction of such works as *Le Pas D'Acier* is not just to interpret the surviving material through historiography, but also to produce an interpretation in practice that is valid in two respects: first, in terms of being true to the work as a whole as distinct from any one performance of it (like the premiere) and second, in terms of exploring and revealing the work's potential for future performances.[11]

In the case of Laban's works both aspects are crucial. Finding the original event 'as a whole' means more than coping with the fabric of the work itself. It includes locating it within its artistic context (Expressionism and Dada) and its wider socio cultural context (the turmoil of the Weimar Republic itself informed by the Wilhelmine romantic period). Locating radical works such as Laban's functions with a double ripple, how the contexts ripple into the work and how the work ripples out to affect the contexts.

Sayers's second point emerges from a perspective on history as a dynamic continuity rather than a series of completed events. This perspective is particularly significant when the engagement is through creating a work anew rather than bringing to the stage a piece that has been preserved in its original form. *Nacht* or *Le Pas d'Acier* presented today will operate in the light of a current double ripple effect, interaction with the artistic and social culture of the 21st century. So too will a work that is re-staged as the original and that can lead to the work being seen as a classic that withstands time or to its being judged as context bound and inevitably old-fashioned. Whether the re-creator and re-stager take account of the cultural changes or not the audience inevitably will. They are alive now and not then. The dancers are trained as they are now not as they were then.

As Martin Hargreaves remarks in the documentary on *Der Schwingende Tempel*: 'Dance is a forgetful art'. As a norm practitioners all but ignore the past and are concerned with making new. But he continues with the view that we must be aware of our past as scholars and choreographers and, from the perspective of Laban scholars, that means practical scholars engaging with the past as a continuity with present practice.

Sayers quotes:

> ...in music Beethoven's *Diabelli Variations*; in the visual arts Pablo Picasso's reworking and transformation of Edouard Manet's paintings or Diego Valesquez' *Las Meninas*, or David Hockney's version of Picasso's *Massacre in Korea* (2003);

11 Preston-Dunlop,V. and Sayers, L-A. 'Gained in Translation: Recreation as Creative Practice' in *Dance Chronicle*, 34:5-45, 2011.

She continues referring to recreations of dance quoting Mats Ek's *Giselle* (1982) or Matthew Bourne's *Swan Lake* (1995) as well as his reworking of other classics. In both these cases the new *Giselle* and the new *Swan Lake* are not historical recreations with the original makers names attached to them but fresh works attributed to Ek and Bourne.

Theatre and opera are expected to give new productions year on year. Where the authenticity and the openness lie seems more clear cut in these art forms. In popular music a lyric and tune are reworked by vocalists in an art form buzzing with re-creativity as they do in the jazz world but in opera and theatre it lies centrally with the written text and written musical score but in many it lies in more than that. A recent production by the English National Opera transcended the line of authenticity in their new production of Benjamin Britten's *A Midsummer Night's Dream* by removing it from a magical forest glade to a doubtful boarding school. Michael White in the *Telegraph*, commenting on the ongoing trend of 'raking over' Britten's sexuality wrote

> I've rarely seen a nastier, more gratuitous example than the new *A Midsummer Night's Dream* that opened last night at ENO.

It would seem that Britten's work lay in more than the text and music. It needed magical context. Of their production of Britten's *Billy Budd* in which the scene is removed from an 18th century sailing warship to 'a Soviet style factory ship', making a nonsense of the references in the text, Ismene Brown of the Arts Hub gave her criticism the headline

> Bloodless, passionless, contextless bore.

Again context did matter.

The age-long discussion in dance has been and is ongoing: where does the authenticity of a dance work lie? With the advent of a workable dance notation and the daily use of film to record a work the concept of authenticity has become a stark issue. Naturally notators and reconstructors have felt the need to defend their system as capable of recording a dance in a manner that can be retrieved by someone else, following the way musical scores are used. But as practice has shown neither a dance score on its own nor a film is sufficient where the work is a product to be reproduced as is. A knowledgeable director is essential. Each dance work offers its own answer. In the case of *Le Pas d'Acier* (1925) the event was never choreographed as intended. The intention lay in the detailed notes made by composer Sergei Prokofiev and set designer Georgi Yakoulov for a Constructivist ballet. The authenticity of a recreation lay in how the total musical/scenographic/ dance event followed the plan in the connected way intended. In the case of Laban's open repertoire, the authenticity lies fundamentally in the processes of his choreography, in the experimental nature of his works and that his

works were made in response to his socio-political context and in line with his overarching mission to secure dance as an independent art form.

Those are the facts and features that as recreators we had to research rigorously and translate into practice in such a way as to 'reveal the work's potential for future performances', the works being *Der Schwingende Tempel, Kammertanz Solos and Duos, Nacht* and *Die Grünen Clowns.*

Chapter Three
Recreating *Der Schwingende Tempel* 1922 as *The Swinging Temple* 2012

The premiere of *Der Schwingende Tempel* in December 1922 was the first performance by the newly formed *Tanzbühne Laban*. **3.1** It took place in Hamburg. With the two other works performed in the same weekend Laban was presenting the world with his vision of how dance theatre might create and serve a dance public at a time when impoverished ballet and touring solo women dancers were the main dance on offer. *Erste Epiche Tanzfolge* (First Epic Dance Sequence) sometimes entitled *Die Geblendeten*, (The Deluded) was a critique of celebrity culture showing what really lay beneath a glittering surface. *Fausts Erlösung* (Faust's Deliverance) was an audacious collaborative treatment of Goethe's famous poem spoken by the city speech choir placed in different levels round the dancers who embodied its spirit 'in movement, rhythm, sculpture and architecture'. It was performed on the huge arena stage, the Ernst Merke Halle (used more recently by the Beatles and Queen).**3.2**

The three performances together certainly had a profound effect on the critic Victor Walther. Speaking of himself as an audience member:

> The soul that is open wants to be seized. It declares itself in support of the new art by which it is enchanted and enflamed, snatched upwards in jubilation and immersed in profound prayer, shattered and broken in pieces. It offers itself completely to that magic by which it feels joy, serene, devout and with a feeling of being drunk with beauty.[1]

He continued later to dismiss 'the era of the façade', in other words ballet, saying it has nothing more to offer and praising Laban for having put the reality 'of the human body back into the service of an art'. The expressivity that Laban's dancers offered must have come as an eye-opener after the traditional performances.

The critic of the *Württemberger Zeitung* summed up the change in dance that he was witnessing with these performances.

> These widely expansive movements are so far removed from the skipping and tripping, strewing of flowers and wafting of veils of the old ballets that we can truly speak of a new language of movement.[2]

---

1 Walther, V. Rudolf von Laban, Reigenspiele by his Tanzbühne on 14th, 17th 18th December 1922 in Herbert Grainer-Mai ed. *Freund und Feind: Kritiken aus Fünf Jahrzehnten.*Weimar und Leipzig. 1980.
2 *Württemberger Zeitung*, undated, trans Virginia Spencer.

The third dance of that December weekend in 1922 was *Der Schwingende Tempel* (The Swinging Temple).[3] **3.3** in Chapter 3. It is this work that we have recreated at Trinity Laban. The dance was reworked by Laban for touring in 1924, titled *Schwingende Gewalten* (Swinging Powers) and recreated a second time with amateurs in 1952 in England, giving three distinct versions. Archival materials on all three exist and it is to those that we turned.

The title of the dance may confuse, for swinging can means something light hearted and that is not what the dance is. What *Schwingende* means in this dance is moving bodies, vibrant, pulsing, alive. Together they create a virtual temple, virtual sacred space. The philosopher of art Susanne Langer when discussing the illusion that particular arts create presented architecture as a 'virtual ethnic domain', a space in which people bound together by a common culture act out their beliefs and duties.[4] That is what Laban set out to convey in *The Swinging Temple*.

The clue to Laban's thinking on the word *Tempel* is to be found in the archives of the 1952 recreation in the document in his hand on 'The real meaning' of the work. Early on he uses the term 'lodge', referring to the Masonic and Rosicrucian lodges that he attended in Paris, in Munich and Zurich. What he is doing, in the 1952 recreation, is placing in the work poietic symbols of Masonic Craft, that is, symbols known to the creator but only available to the viewer by being told they are there.[5] From the explanatory text *The Meaning of Masonry*:

> I cannot too strongly impress upon you, Brethren, the fact that, throughout our rituals and our lectures, the references made to the Lodge are not to the building in which we meet. That building itself is intended to be but a symbol, a veil of allegory concealing something else... The real Lodge referred to throughout our rituals is our own individual personalities.

The writer continues:

> Man himself is a Lodge. And just as the Masonic Lodge is 'an assemblage of brethren and fellows met to expatiate upon the mysteries of the Craft,' so individual man is a composite being made up of various properties and faculties assembled together in him with a view to their harmonious interaction and working out the purpose of life.[6]

The word Lodge, if Laban were to use it in the title of the dance, would state

---

3 The 1952 instantiation in England directed by Lisa Ullmann has *The Swinging Cathedral* as title. In our recreation of 2012 we return to 'temple' with its more all-embracing association over time of a sacred space.

4 Langer, S. *Feeling and Form*. New York: Charles Scribner's Sons. 1953, p.95.

5 Semiotic theory of musicologist J.J.Nattiez. *Music and Discourse*, Princeton University Press. 1970.

6 Wilmshurst, W.L. *The Meaning of Masonry*. New York: Barnes and Noble. 1999, pp.33 and 91.

overtly that his source was Masonic so he did not. 'Temple' is a universal enough term for a sacred building.

Laban, in referring to dance and movement as 'living architecture', uses the term in the sense that architecture, as he knew from his studies in Paris, had clear functional laws that ensured that a building would not fall down but also that it would be so devised and proportioned as to say more than its bricks and mortar, say something about its purpose and the people for whom it was intended.[7] In *Der Schwingende Tempel* 1922 the architecture was a well-proportioned dance and the temple an assemblage of 'Brethren', in this case his committed company members. The overarching theme of the work was to present 'individual personalities', and celebrate the possibility of their 'harmonious interaction'.

Concerning the 1922 version, the chapter in Laban's autobiography called *The Swinging Temple* leads up to this statement:

> Behind external events the dancer perceives another entirely different world. There is an energy behind all occurrences and material things for which it is almost impossible to find a name. A hidden forgotten landscape lies there, the land of silence, the realm of the soul, and in the centre of this land stands the swinging temple.[8]

That places the dance in 'the land of silence'. He goes on:

> ....a few words about this strange land. In the jungles and deserts of our planet man can be strangled and devoured by giant snakes and tigers. He can die of thirst or suffocate from heat, freeze to death in the cold of the north or south or suffer other disasters. Is it less perilous for travellers in the land of silence? Is it easy to pioneer its exploration? Crossing the borderline may lead to conflict with one's fellows left behind. The keen air which one brings back is only partly accepted.[9]

While that can be read as wild musing, for Laban it was quite straightforward. It is what happens to dancers who integrate mind, spirit and body as they create and dance. They transcend into the land of silence as an all-embracing experience. Musicians may transcend in a similar way but Laban believed that dance offers the strongest and most direct experience. In *The Swinging Temple* he focused on the realm of the soul with its hopes and fears, ecstasies and despondencies, conflicts and resolutions, for the dancers and, through images and dynamic dancing, for his spectators. The *Tanzbühne* performances were so strong because the dancers in his group were bound together by their belief in his all-consuming mission for dance, his quest. Their belief was thrown into the dance in true Expressionistic style.

In the archival materials of the 1922 performance his choreographic

7 Laban, R. ed L. Ullmann. *Choreutics*. London, McDonald &Evans 1966, p.5.
8 Laban, 1935, p.89.
9 Laban, 1935, p.90.

method, his sound score, the rhythm and spatial forms of the colours, are there, all in hastily written documents in Laban's hand. **3.4** Notes on the work refer to Goethe's writings on colour theory. Laban uses six colours in the dance as a metaphor for archetypal temperaments, white, black, yellow, blue, green, red. While it is hardly original to use costume colour to convey characteristics in ballets Laban goes much further than some other choreographers. From the materials in the archives of the 1952 performance he is quite specific in how he considers each of the six colours in terms of their dynamic qualities and in terms of the way the dancers of each colour interact with each other. The red dancers work collaboratively, the blue dancers depend on each other, the yellow dancers meet and part, the black dancers confront the other colours in unison, the green dancers surround and entwine, the white dancers work in calm unison.

There are almost no archives of the 1924 instantiation except the programme notes and newspaper reports. The *Tanzbühne* was attempting to tour in a time of acute financial inflation. They could not afford to take the whole company so transformed their repertoire into sections that can be danced by a smaller company while maintaining the main thrust of the works. The colours are there, their interaction is there but with a smaller cast and not assembled as a continuous evening-long work. The word Temple is no longer there. There is no setting of a sacred space. Laban is being economic. He is using material already in the dancers bodies as particularly strong *divertissement*. The spectators will still have a varied performance to arouse a range of responses but no overt journey into the land of silence.

The 1952 performance was quite different, a revival directed by Lisa Ullmann with Diana Jordan and Sylvia Bodmer (a performer in the original) as collaborators. The occasion was a summer school of the Modern Dance Holiday Courses, a main vehicle for supplementing the training of teachers of Laban's Modern Educational Dance as well as being open to any interested person. The participants were not trained dancers but were familiar with and enthusiastic about Laban's creative methods. The event was not an attempt to recreate the whole work but to concentrate on the contrasting qualities of the colour groups. It was never intended as a public performance but danced in the spirit of 'dance for all'.[10]

The 1952 archives showed that modern piano pieces had been found for each colour where in the original the sound score of piano and percussion was created and improvised as a response to the movement. This is a surprising decision artistically speaking since Laban was so strongly taking dance out of dependence on music. Possibly limited time and dancer inexperience made it necessary. On locating the pieces (by Kodaly, Prokofiev,

10 Private conversation with Marion North who was a participant in the 1952 Summer School.

Rusiki and others) they gave us a good sense of the tempo and dynamic level that Ullmann had worked towards. Notated fragments of the 'leit motifs' of each colour were there. The notation was elementary but gave some sense of what the motifs were.

As recreators of the work with professionally trained dancers in London in 2012 we started from a position that was radically different from all three versions. Our dancers were technically able from daily classes in ballet and various contemporary techniques. They had encountered Choreological Studies, the contemporary development of Laban's original choreology. Melanie Clarke, the rehearsal director, shared a eukinetic and choreutic language with the dancers so communication was easy. They had experience of making work themselves and of having work made on and with them. But they were not used to Expressionism, unlike their 1922 compatriots who were steeped in it. The 1952 dancers had no technical training behind them but they had direct knowledge and devotion to Laban's ideas on dynamics and space. In a sense they were nearer being 'Brethren' than our 2012 dancers.

The rehearsals for the *Tanzbühne*'s 1922 programme took place in rural Gleschendorf, outside because they had no hall to work in, in 'a meadow with thistles' according to Sylvia Bodmer. You can see from the photograph of their training that their commitment and vigour and daring was profound. They were expressionists. In the second image at Gleschendorf, Laban is leading with drum in hand as he instructs his dancers in the creative use of percussion and in guiding them to find all manner of rhythms that will end up in *The Swinging Temple*. **3.5, 3.6**

The notes in Laban's hand show his clarification of the dancers' rhythms and phrasing and the sound to go with them. These are instructions for the pianist Richard Goldschmid and percussionist Friedrich Wilckens whose task was to follow the dancers' lead. **3.7**

Melanie Clarke's experience of Laban work was as a practising notator. Recently she had reconstructed from the score Yvonne Rainer's *Trio A*. It is hard to imagine a work more contrasted to Expressionism than *Trio A*. She was also a faculty member in the Choreological Studies department, a Release Technique teacher as well as being a choreographer of her own post post modern work.

Clarke and I met over a three months research period to study the copious material and develop a rehearsal plan. We decided to bring together those elements of each instantiation that were constant and collate them into a similar structure to the 1922 piece, but condensed. What Laban spread over twenty minutes for each topic we condensed into five. Because Clarke had never worked with me before on a recreation we spent considerable time together in the studio working through possible embodiments of each scene. In that way I could share with her my 'living archive' knowledge. I had to pass on what I knew from Sylvia Bodmer, Kurt Jooss and Albrecht Knust, all dancers in the original, and my own years with Laban. While that included straightforward material such as the scales and rings in space it also included his collaborative choreographic method, how his quest translates in the studio, how his attitude to his dancers works in a rehearsal and how to engage the dancers with the spirit and techniques of Expressionism.

We were limited to twenty-five minutes performance time where the original was a whole evening's work. We had thirty hours of studio time over two weeks in total while Laban had from June to December of 1922, albeit on a meadow. Melanie Clarke tells the reader of her experience.

Melanie Clarke's perspective as rehearsal director

This recreation process would not be the first but the third. It was originally created in 1922 and Laban himself produced two subsequent recreations in 1924 and 1952. Laban remade, reformed, adapted his work for each instantiation. Although he worked for and discovered a new vocabulary of movement and ways of generating it using his choreutic and eukinetic theories, it seems that his sense of the identity of his work was centered in the content – the structures, scenarios, characters and meaning, rather than the specific details of the movements. His choreographic approach was more inclined towards setting tasks for his dancers to fulfill using the understanding of movement he had taught them. As Rita Zabekow remembered; 'He saw choreography evolving and he moved himself, allowing people to improvise.'[11] The evolution of the work often continued as he re-made and adapted works to fit a new set of circumstances. Thus when re-staging work he retained the generative approach and the significance of the meaning of the work rather than the movement's form. So for the 2012 recreation we set out to do the same. This involved two major things: discovering and drawing conclusions about what is the identity of *Der Schwingende Tempel* (*The Swinging Temple*) – what are the essential features that made all three versions of the work *Der Schwingende Tempel* rather than three completely different works; and then enabling a group of post post modern conservatoire trained young dancers to manifest it.

Our aim was to uncover the significant features of the choreography and then to find movement solutions using Laban's praxis. Using the information from the gathered written sources, a structure was found that would encompass the full sense of the journey of the work within the limitations established for the project. We were not trying to breathe new life into old steps (as one might do when reconstructing a dance work from a notated

---

11 McCaw, D. (ed) *The Laban Sourcebook*. New York: Routledge, 2011, p. 118

score perhaps) but using the rediscovered understanding of the life of the work to inspire its regeneration. Thus the process of recreating *The Swinging Temple* was one of finding the overarching themes, significant features and structures that were present in all three of Laban's versions to discover its identity. There were differences in the numbers of dancers and the length of the three versions of *The Swinging Temple* but certain significant aspects of the work became readily apparent, the division of the dancers into colour temperaments and the structure of the journey of the work. We devised four scenes each with transitional sections:

Scene One: *The Land of Silence*
Scene Two: *Celebration of Difference*
Scene Three: *Work*
Scene Four: *Harmony*

Scene One was about setting a sacred space in which the narrative could unfold. **3.8, 3.9** Scene Two revealed the different temperaments by juxtaposing them beside each other. Scene Three saw the subjugation of the differences between the temperaments by the domination of the Black temperament and Scene Four would bring a resolution through a harmonious integration of all. This is how the plan looked:

Scene One
Setting the primordial sacred space, 'land of silence', give way to primordial chaos.
          Transition: emerging differences
Scene Two
Celebration of range of human temperaments, co-existing but neither collaborating nor confronting. Red and Yellow, then Blue and Green, then Black and White. **3.10-3.16**
          Transition: Black dominate. White withdraw
Scene Three
Individual temperament overcome by urban materialism, loss of identity and group cohesion, pain of mechanisation, competition leading to groups struggling as the systems break down, dehumanisation
          Transition: groups squashed together and tussling. **3.17**
Scene Four
Gradual transformation led by White towards possibility of collaboration in harmony, celebration and reaching for the cosmos **3.18-3.20**
Coda Five
Brief reiteration of sacred space, departure **3.21 – 3.22**

Once we had compiled our strands and sub-strands, our set of essential features needed to be brought to life as dance. Laban uses the word Swinging to mean animated, alive. He wrote:

> Dance is all culture, all sociability. Dance is the swinging force which relates intangible conceptions to religion... the purest image of the dance of dances, of universal happening, is the round dance [Reigen] in which the human body swings.[12]

Furthermore, he relates the idea of Swinging to the harmonic laws of movement that exist within the shared harmonic laws of all life as well as crystallography and the cosmos. Thus, for recreating *The Swinging Temple* we needed to attempt to rediscover 'the harmonic movement swingings of the human body' (McCaw 2011, p.64) that brought this work to life.

Laban believed in the lived experience of dance as research. He claimed that:

> Although in analysis we look at movement from the standpoint of an outside observer, we should try to feel it sympathetically from within. A mind trained to assist bodily perspective, instead of combating it, would give us a completely new outlook on movement.[13]

As a dancer and teacher of release-based technique my approach to my other roles as a choreologist and Labanotator is from a body-based perspective; I use a phenomenological methodology of direct experiencing through my body to gain insight into my object of study, similar to Laban's method, as McCaw (2011) states:

> It is again the actual experience of the practice of dancing itself that Laban is mainly interested in.[14]

For the recreation of *The Swinging Temple* I used moving as my way to understand the work as part of Laban's aesthetic. Here I relied a lot on reflective discussions with Preston-Dunlop. Preston-Dunlop is a living embodiment of Laban's dance training methods and aesthetic and thus is an ambassador of his artistic vision. Hence, in our practical research process, Preston-Dunlop became my aesthetic warden. This methodology enabled the aesthetic guardianship of Preston-Dunlop to keep me from the temptations of a practised ideosyncratic post post modern approach.

The practice of archeochoreology as research is to re-find the past thus there needs to be a significant and visible attachment to a historical era as well as adhering to the structures and content of choreographic intention. Although there is no denying that whatever we produced would be a product of now, the context of this recreation was to provide a link to the past both for the audience and (significantly) for the dancers. I needed to find a way to

12 McCaw, 2011, p.53.
13 Laban, 1966, p.90.
14 McCaw, 2011, p.57.

connect the dancers to a way of moving and approaching dance that allowed them access to a physical relationship to the era and Laban's approach. As Laban's training method is one of promoting awareness and understanding of movement this embodied understanding of their dance heritage would enable them to use their creativity as Laban's own dancers did to fulfill the concepts of the work. As McCaw states about Laban's own processes, the aim was to discover 'a feeling for form, in terms of the experience of the dancer herself'.[15] So, I worked through my body first in order to discover what sort of experiences I needed to generate for the dancers so they too could discover this work as an Expressionist danced experience and be active in its recreation. Like myself it would be simpler perhaps for the dancers to re-invent *The Swinging Temple* with a post post modern artist aesthetic thus, part of our approach to the recreation involved embodying Laban's aesthetics.

As part of the practical research process I performed Laban's scales not as a series of spatial destinations and pathways for creative exploration but as a way of embodying the Laban movement style as he and his followers taught it and as Preston-Dunlop learnt it from Lisa Ullmann under the watching oversight of Laban himself. The highly physical full-bodied pathways of motion through spatial patterns gives rise to the powerful energy of the aesthetic. No shy or sly subtlety or irony here, movement is statement, not suggestion, with no apology. The movement is not about isolation and there is no hierarchy of body parts; actions are full bodied, utilising all of the inter-connected and integrated body: As Walter Bodmer wrote in his diary in 1952 after working with Laban as a young man:

> We were taught harmonic movements and movement sequences designed to exercise all parts of the body to their fullest extent.[16]

The style of movement was made to practise dance as a process of engaging 'a person's body, mind and spirit'[17] as an integrated and empowered whole. As Laban stated in *Choreutics*, 'The integrating power of movement is perhaps its most important value for the individual.'[18] Thus, through practising this type of action, with the fullness of understanding and intent, an empowered and vital being emerges.

This mode of understanding Laban's work through a kinetic training was then carried through as a significant part of the recreation process with the dancers. I used the structures and principles of Laban's praxis to create a dance class that was a specific training for the recreation. This process of training in the aesthetic of Laban's work in the way of a technique is not

---

15 McCaw, 2011, p.58.
16 McCaw, 2011, p.xviii.
17 McCaw, 2011, p.45.
18 Laban, 1966, p.112.

3.1 *Der Schwingende Tempel*, Tanzbühne Laban press photo, Hamburg, 1922.
Photographer John Thiele.

Deutſche Bühne E. V.,
Bühnengemeinde Hamburg

Reigenſpiele der Tanzbühne
RUDOLF VON LABAN
14. bis 16. Dezember   Ernst Merckhalle

„Fausts Erlösung“
(nach Motiven aus Goethes Faust 2. Teil).
Sechs Reigen

Leitung der Sprechchöre: Am Flügel:
Vilma Möndeberg   Richard Goldschmied

Gestaltung der Bühneneinrichtung E. C.Thomassow v. Deutſch. Schauspielhaus
Bechsteinflügel aus der Niederlage Eduard Otto
Beleuchtung Firma Carl Stuhr

1. Reigen:
　　Die Tänzer: Sonnenkreise, Erwachen
　　Die Sprecher: „Faust“ 2. Teil, 1. Akt
　　　Szene: Dämmerung　　　Ariel - Chor - Faust

2. Reigen:
　　Musikalische Einleitung
　　Die Sprecher: „Faust“ 2. Teil, 1. Akt
　　　Szene: Weitläufiger Saal mit Nebengemächern,
　　　　Herold.

　　Die Tänzer: Carneval
　　Die Sprecher: Aus obiger Szene während der
　　　Tänze: Zoilo-Thersites, nach dem Tanz: Plutus

3. Reigen:
　　Die Tänzer: Antiker Reigen
　　Die Sprecher: „Faust“ 2. Teil,
　　　3. Akt: Schluß der Helena-Szene
　　　　(vierteiliger Chor)

P A U S E

3.2 Programme of *Fausts Erlösung* [Faust's salvation]. Hamburg, 1922.

Die Sprecher: Aus „Faust" 2. Teil 5. Akt,
Szene: Weiter Ziergarten, großer gerade-
geführter Kanal,　Tiefe Nacht: Lynkeus der
der Türmer. Am Schluss nach den Tänzen,
aus der Szene Mitternacht: Faust (erblindet)
Die Tänzer: Tat und Sorge.

5. Reigen :
Die Tänzer: Lemurentänze, Teufelstänze.
Die Sprecher: (zwischen den Tänzen).
„Faust" 2. Teil 5. Akt, Szene: Vorhof des
Palastes, Grablegung. Fausts letzte Worte,
Mephisto, Engel.

6. Reigen:
Die Sprecher: Aus „Faust" 2. Teil 5. Akt die
letzte Szene: Bergschluchten, Felseneinöde
Die Tänzer: Verklärung

Mitwirkende:

Vortänzer:	Gertrud Löser
Hochtänzer:	Bereska, Keith, Knust, Mené, Neggo, Oesterreich, Roon, Therwal.
Mitteltänzer:	Feist, Löser, Mampoteng, Müller, Nurk, Schek, Volcard, Wehnert.
Tieftänzer:	Bodmer, El-Corret, Frank, Küpper, Troplowitz, Urian, Volta.

Trommler, Sprecher.

Wiederholungen von „Fausts Erlösung"
15. und 16. Dezember, 7½ Uhr, Ernst Merckhalle
„Der schwingende Tempel" 18., 19. und 20. Dezember
CONVENTGARTEN
„I. Epische Tanzfolge" 17., 21. und 22. Dezember
CONVENTGARTEN

Für Inhaber der Reihenkarten zum 14., 17. und 20. Dezember weisen wir
darauf hin, daß am 17. (Sonntag-vorm.) die „1. Epische Tanzfolge" und am
20. Dezember „Der schwingende Tempel" aufgeführt werden.

Karten zu allen Veranstaltungen sind zu haben
Deutsche Bühne, Holsenplatz 1, in den bekannten Vorverkaufsstellen und an
den Abendkassen

---

*Die 1. Jahresausgabe der Deutschen Bühne E. V. (Unsere Theaterkultur-
Bestrebungen) liegt am Eingang des Saales aus. Preis M. 100,—
(im Buchhandel etwa M. 400,—)*

3.2 continued

Deutfche Bühne E. V.,
Bühnengemeinde Hamburg

Reigenfpiele der Tanzbühne
RUDOLF   VON   LABAN
18., 19., 20. Dezember   Conventgarten
DER SCHWINGENDE
TEMPEL.

Vier Reigen

Begleitende Klangspiele: Am Flügel:
Friedrich Wilckens   Richard Goldschmied

Gestaltung der Bühneneinrichtung E. C. Thomassow v. Deutsch. Schauspielhaus

Bechsteinflügel aus der Niederlage Eduard Otto

Beleuchtung Firma Carl Stuhr

Kostüme: Entwurf von Laban, Ausführung Kitty Suiter

Im Vorreigen wird die chaotische Bewegung der
Schwarzen, Roten, Gelben und Blauen durch die
Harmonie der Weissen und Grünen abgelöst. Im 1.
Reigen, der ohne Unterbrechung einsetzt, verlodert
Chaos und Harmonie in bacchantischem Aufschwung.

Der zweite Reigen bringt eine Versöhnung der
Farbengruppen, die im rhythmisierten Wettstreit,
dessen Gipfel die Männertänze sind, zur Ermattung
und zu tändelndem Spiel zweier Kreise führt und im
Zwiespalt endet.

P A U S E

Eine bizarre aber straffe Harmonisierung erfährt
das Raumspiel im 3. Reigen; diese wird jäh durch
eine Groteske unterbrochen und der Reigen schließt
in trauriger Feierlichkeit.

3.3 Programme for the premiere of *Der Schwingende Tempel*. Hamburg 1922.

Die Entwicklung der Raumordnungen führt im 4. Reigen über Auschaltung mancher traumhafter, letzter Disharmonien zu einer Bändigung durch Regelmässigkeit, in der sich Individuelles und Absolutes vereinigt.

Die Weißen: Mine Mampoteng, Lucie Mené, Ingeborg Roon, Mario Volcard, Reigenführer

Die Schwarzen: Sylvia Bodmer, Reigenführer,   El Corret. Gido Larass, Wehnert.

    (führende Gruppen im Vorreigen und Finale)

Die Roten: (führende Gruppe im 1. Reigen): Khadven Joos, Reigenführer, Hildegard Troplowitz, Ida Urian, Fini Volta.

Die Gelben: (führende Gruppe im 2. Reigen): Jens Keiths, Reigenführer, Gerd Neggo, Gertrud Löser, Claire Therval

Die Grünen: (führende Gruppe im 4. Reigen): Dussia Bereska, Reigenführer, Gerda Schek, Edgar Frank Lotte Müller.

Die Blauen: (führende Gruppe im 4. Reigen): Herta Feist, Reigenführer, Albrecht Knust, Helmi Nurk, Laura Oesterreich.

Trommler.

Wiederholungen von
„Der schwingende Tempel"
19. und 20. Dezember, 7½ Uhr, Conventgarten

„Erſte epiſche Tanzfolge"   21. und 22. Dezember, 7½ Uhr CONVENTGARTEN

Karten zu allen Veranstaltungen sind zu haben
Deutsche Bühne, Holsenplatz 1, in den bekannten Vorverkaufsstellen und an den Abendkassen

Die 1. Jahresausgabe der Deutschen Bühne E. V. (Unsere Theaterkultur-Bestrebungen) liegt am Eingang des Saales aus. Preis M. 100,—

3.3 continued

3.4 Rudolf Laban's group floor plan sketches for *Der Schwingende Tempel.* 1922.

3.5 Tanzbühne Laban rehearsing at Gleschendorf, 1922.

3.6 Rudolf Laban teaching the men's group of the Tanzbühne Laban,

3.7 Laban's sketch of the rhythms of movement and music, instructions for the musicians.

3.8 *The Swinging Temple 2012.* Setting the sacred space of *The Land of Silence*. Photographer Peter Sayers.

3.9 *The Swinging Temple 2012.* Creating the swinging temple in *The Land of Silence*. Photographer Peter Sayers.

3.10 *The Swinging Temple 2012. Celebration of Difference*: Red temperament. Photographer Peter Sayers.

3.11 *The Swinging Temple 2012. Celebration of Difference*: Red temperament. Photographer Kyle Stevenson.

3.12 *The Swinging Temple 2012. Celebration of Difference*: Blue and Green temperaments. Photographer Peter Sayers.

3.13 *The Swinging Temple 2012. Celebration of Difference*: Green temperament. Photographer Kyle Stevenson.

3.14 *The Swinging Temple 2012. Celebration of Difference*: Yellow temperament.
Photographer Kyle Stevenson.

3.15 *The Swinging Temple 2012. Celebration of Difference*: Black temperament. Photographer Peter Sayers.

3.16 *The Swinging Temple 2012. Celebration of Difference*: Black and White temperaments. Photographer Peter Sayers.

3.17 *The Swinging Temple 2012*. The tussle of the temperaments.
Photographer Peter Sayers.

3.18 *The Swinging Temple 2012*. *Harmony*, dimensional counterpoint.
Photographer Peter Sayers.

3.19 *The Swinging Temple 2012* . *Harmony*, 7-ring counterpoint. Photographer Peter Sayers

3.20 *The Swinging Temple 2012*. *Harmony*, White leading the A scale canon. Photographer Kyle Stevenson.

3.21 *The Swinging Temple 2012*. Praise. Photographer Peter Sayers.

3.22 *The Swinging Temple 2012*. Reiteration of The Temple.
Photographer Kyle Stevenson.

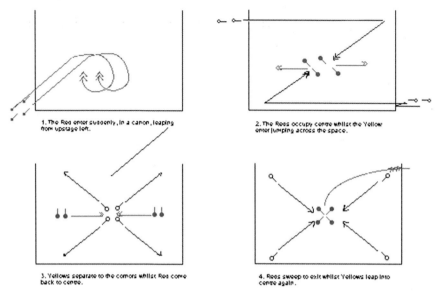

The Swinging Temple 2012: Scene Two: Celebration of Difference, Red and Yellow

1. The Red enter suddenly, in a canon, leaping from upstage left.

2. The Reds occupy centre whilst the Yellow enter jumping across the space.

3. Yellows separate to the corners whilst Red come back to centre.

4. Reds sweep to exit whilst Yellows leap into centre again.

3.23 *The Swinging Temple 2012*. Melanie Clarke's floor plans for *The Celebration of Difference*, White and Black.

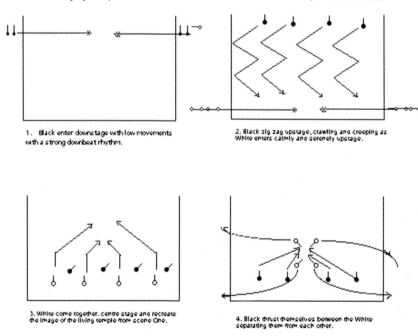

The Swinging Temple 2012: Scene Two: Celebration of Difference, White and Black

1. Black enter downstage with low movements with a strong downbeat rhythm.

2. Black zig zag upstage, crawling and creeping as White enters calmly and serenely upstage.

3. White come together, centre stage and recreate the image of the living temple from scene One.

4. Black thrust themselves between the White separating them from each other.

3.24 *The Swinging Temple 2012*. Melanie Clarke's floor plans for *The Celebration of Difference*, Red and Yellow.

3.25 *The Swinging Temple 2012*. Robert Coleridge's score for setting the sacred space.

3.26 *The Swinging Temple 2012.* Robert Coleridge's score for the opening of *Harmony*.

3.27 *The Swinging Temple 2012.* Robert Coleridge's score for a transition in *Harmony.*

a common aspect of learning Laban's praxis. Laban wasn't interested in creating a codified technique as others did; again in *Choreutics* he claims that:

> Individual styles, although in an art form of utmost importance, should never become standardised rules for general use.[19]

He was interested in enabling creative artistic expression through an acquired embodied awareness of movement. His aim was to foster understanding of space and quality of expression rather than set steps; Laban wrote:

> Next to the Art of Dancing there is dance technique. A lot of what is called dance is inartistic gymnastics, acrobatics, posing, pretension, eroticism and the like.[20]

Nevertheless, he did train dancers but allowed the system of doing so to be open and evolve as his ideas changed and developed, the focus always on the expressivity of the art form. These ideas about movement as an educational activity have been remembered and carried on rather than a specified practice of exercises or choreographed steps.

Laban's dancers were sometimes criticised for not being enough trained technically. The Ballet community at the time looked upon Laban's dancers with 'a derogatory eye' because their movement aesthetic did not conform to the

> narrow band of aesthetics of the body, of line, of dynamics, of musicality acceptable to the traditional ballet advocate.[21]

This differs from the perspective within the setting of a current contemporary conservatoire like Trinity Laban in that dancers are expected to have open technical skills that can be adapted to a variety of movement styles. The twenty-four young dancers in this current recreation had diverse technical skill but perhaps needed to find the rawness of expression and daring of the *Tanzbühne*. So, following on from the recreation practice of my colleague Alison Curtis-Jones in her recreations of *Green Clowns* and *Nacht,* I created a technique class in a format that the dancers would be familiar with but based it on exploring Laban's praxis honed within the context of *The Swinging Temple.* I made use of the spatial scales as a major feature of this class, starting with exploring the Dimensional Scales and the planes using different qualities, then moving on to the 3 Rings, A Scale, Diagonal Scale and 7 Rings. These particular scales were used in the class as we had decided to use them for Scene Four of the choreography to embody the harmony in the resolution of the work. The scales became the way of embodying

---

19 Laban, 1966, p.50.
20 McCaw, 2011, p.46.
21 Preston-Dunlop, V. & Lahusen, S. eds. *Schrifttanz: A View of Dance in the Weimar Republic.* London: Dance Books. 1990, p.4.

'the harmonic movement swingings of the human body'[22] and encapsulate Laban's intention for the end of this work. The feeling of harmony rather than unison was practised through performing the scales in duets of harmonic opposition. So these scales became three-fold in significance: a technical training exercise, a way of understanding and embodying the aesthetic, and a practice for performing the recreated choreography.

The Swinging Temple is often thought of as Laban's most abstract work as the dancers become symbols rather than human characters. Dörr [23] quotes the review in the *Hamburger Nachrichten*, (December 19 1922)

> This abstract choreography... presented 'the gradual transformation of disharmony into harmony, of chaos into cosmos' by means of colour, form, and movement.

This meant that the meaning needed to be embodied in the dance and thus, the movement needed to be created specifically. It was decided not to reconstruct the notated extracts from the 1952 version of *The Swinging Temple* as we had not set out to reconstruct the 1952 version but recreate the essence of the work from all three versions. Our aim, as Lesley-Anne Sayers states about her recreation of *Le Pas d'Acier* in 2004 , was to create a

> rich experience of the work, layered by multidimensional (and time-lapse) understandings of it.[24]

So the notated extracts became a resource to understand better the nature of the temperaments as they were, in one instance, manifested in movements. Despite being known for his successful notation system, Laban used this resource to share ideas among his dancers/collaborators within the creative process rather than produce recordings of his own works for posterity, so the notations were short extracts under the titles of the colours but no context of when and where or how they were used is recorded. I reconstructed the extracts so that I could, through my embodiment, feel the essence of the character of each colour and see how the sensing of the movement corresponded to written descriptions of the work in order to define for ourselves the significant features that needed to be present for the six temperaments in a new instantiation.

From a whole combination of resources a list of characteristics for each temperament emerged. I include in the figure below Effort terminology despite the fact that Effort did not appear in Laban's language until his time in England. According to his description of dynamics in *Choreographie* (1926)

22 McCaw, 2011, p.64.

23 Dörr, E. *Rudolf Laban: the Dancer of the Crystal*. USA: Scarecrow Press, Inc. 2008, p.98.

24 Preston-Dunlop, V. & Sayers, L. A. Gained in Translation: Recreation as Creative Practice, *Dance Chronicle*, 34:5-45, Routledge, 2011, p.35.

colour	images	Choreutics	Eukinetics	Rhythm
RED	devouring fierceness of fire;	Sudden appearance, sweeping curves	slash (flexible, sudden, strong)	fast 3/4 with accents on different parts of each bar
YELLOW	spreading the brightness of outgoing movements all over the stage; jumps, leaps, skips	straight lines. spoke like. parting and meeting.	direct, light,	fast 2/4 jumping rhythm
BLACK	animal spirit and dark powers	low, crawling, creeping.	punch (sudden, strong, direct)	10 beat strong pulse driven rhythm
WHITE	priest-like' bringers of peace; solemn, slow, scooping and strewing.	straight lines, the dimensions, the planes	sustained, direct,	slow 4/4 regular paced rhythm
GREEN	organic plant life entwining, organic, growing	twists and spirals	flexible, impulsive (deceleration)	free timing using impulsive phrasing
BLUE	mist turning to ice. freezing and melting. Sadness, funeral procession.	Drifting undulations and tableaux	Floating (sustained, flexible, light) changing to bound and sudden	free timing with actions shifting between continuous flow, to stillnesses and then sudden punctuations.

he referred to impulse, impact, swing, vibration, light, strong, and weak. By the 1952 archive of *The Swinging Temple* the effort qualities are there but not before, however the effort terminology is understood by all the collaborators on the project and became a means of sharing our understanding of the qualities that arose from the images and written descriptions in the archives. The rhythms and time signatures arose from the 1922 archive of *Laban's rhythm score.*

Using these identified features we started to explore manifesting them in motion. This process obviously involves an interpretive act as there is always a gap between written descriptions and analytical notions about movement, and moving. However, this interpretive act was held within the tight parameters of the structure and meaning of the work alongside the practised embodied aesthetic and again under the aesthetic guardianship of Preston-Dunlop. The research process involved the practice of embodiment and then our reflections and discussion to hone this interpretation.

The dancers then explored these six temperaments as part of the warm up class. Watching the dancers embody the distinct phrases allowed the work to be cast through seeing which dancers resonated with the six distinct temperaments. Laban's use and belief in individualisation made casting according to the individual character of the dancers important. As Preston-Dunlop states:

> Individual differences mattered... Laban cherished the movement voice of each member of his *Kammertanzbühne*.[25]

The dancers, once cast, were then given floor plans and rhythms to create material for their colour based on the felt experience of the temperaments. Floor patterns were a feature of the versions of *The Swinging Temple* with larger casts and the colours had different uses of the general space as part of their differentiation from each other. Pathways and structures for the colours in general space were devised from written descriptions and drawings and then notated for each temperament. These notated floor plans therefore led the dancers creative explorations rather than resulted from the movement. **3.23, 3.24** The floor plans also meant that when juxtaposed together in the space two colours would move around each other in particular ways. For example, the reds travelled in sweeping curves to occupy centre stage but then separate into stage right and stage left duos allowing the yellows, travelling in straight diagonals, to converge in the centre.

I created tasks within the warm-up class to enable the dancers to practise embodying different qualities of motion and vocalisations. It soon became clear that certain qualities were more practised for them than others and also that to fully express effort qualities through the whole integrated body took a considerable amount of energy. The dancers found the embodiment of Strong hard to achieve even though they were strong in their bodies. This may be connected to the fact that dance techniques today generally use strength but don't express strength. Use of the sensorial motion factor of Force as an expressive energy is often manifested in today's technique practices as an understanding of weight and heaviness rather than strength.

This exploration of strength was particularly relevant for several parts of the recreation. Energetic fullness in the body was required for Scene One in which the dancers needed to find a powerful presence with a sense of anticipation and wonder for the opening and then an almost primitive strength and power as they pounded the ground for setting the sacred space.

---

25 Preston-Dunlop, V. & Sayers, L-A., 2011, p.15.

Chapter Four
Recreating the *Kammertanzbühne Laban*
Solos and Duos

The idea for a small dance group making varied short works came, according to Laban, from his right hand assistant Dussia Bereska.[1] **4.1**

> The idea of founding a chamber dance theatre and giving it a particular name came from my brave and inspired colleague, the one who had helped with the organisation and training of the group [Tanzbühne Laban].

Bereska became the director of the *Kammertanzbühne Laban* from its inception in 1923 but it was not until late 1924 that it took its most productive and unique form. Several factors led to its constitution.

The large company, the *Tanzbühne Laban*, had found themselves stranded in Zagreb in June 1924 while on their first tour of the Balkans. Laban hoped to show his work in his own ethnic corner of Europe in a tour that started playing to acclaim in the main theatres in Leipzig, Prague, Graz and Halberstadt. They ran out of money because the catastrophic inflation had reduced the value of the German Mark for foreign exchange. The company included almost all the first group who had joined Laban as soon as he began working in Germany in 1920. They were highly skilled and committed men and women. With no money to go on to Belgrade nor to get back to Hamburg as a company, they split up. Laban had to get to Halle where the first movement choir for children run by ex-student Jenny Gertz was performing and then back to Hamburg for the premiere of his movement choir work *Agamemnons Tod* (Death of Agamemnon) rehearsed in his absence.

Bereska made for Rome, taking four of the most experienced dancers with her Jens Keith, Edgar Frank, Hildegard Troplowitz and Ingeborg Roon. She set up as a performing group there, *Balletto Laban*, and started a school. But it was not successful. Italy had just become a unified country and the Italians considered it essential to establish a national culture that was totally their own. Anything German or French was shunned so Bereska had chosen an impossible moment to establish Laban's work there. She returned to Hamburg with her group and, ever creative and resourceful, suggested running the *Kammertanzbühne Laban* as a Hamburg version of *Balletto Laban*.

4.2 4.3 What made the *Kammertanz* development unique to that moment was the financial situation of the city of Hamburg, affected by inflation and, amongst other problems, unable to pay for the zoo. The zoo, just down the road from Schwanenwik where the Laban school and headquarters were

---

1 All the quotations on the *Kammertanzbühne* methods come from Laban, 1935, pp.106-109.

housed, gave Laban an opportunity. He was invited to use the main halls in the zoological gardens, empty and forlorn, as a performing space. The authorities thought that dancing as lively and youthful as *Der Schwingende Tempel* might attract people in and once there they might remember how they loved seeing the animals and support the zoo. The irony of the invitation was not lost on Laban, However:

> I made a contract with the zoo management and asked for a hall to be adapted as a theatre, and this was carried out precisely according to my specifications... A considerable number of subscribers came to visit our regular performances... Ours was the first and the only specialised dance-theatre.

The particulars of this opportunity had enormous influence on what kind of dance theatre Laban and Bereska would generate. First, it was a resident company performing several times a week to subscribers who came again and again. There being no such thing as television, almost no radio, no CDs, no Internet, people normally went out for their nightly entertainment. Therefore the company had to produce new dances continuously to provide for the unusual phenomenon of regular spectators.

> An audience will only be attracted to attend a dance-theatre regularly and maintain its interest if there is diversity in what is offered – something we possessed at that happy and fruitful time – and also if the particular types of dance are carefully articulated and arranged.

Diversity was the key to their success. They concentrated on four types of dance that Laban named as 'ornamental, ecstatic, grotesque' plus popular national dances. 'Ornamental' covered any dance that was primarily just lovely to watch, that would give straightforward aesthetic pleasure. 'Ecstatic' covered dances that transported the viewer into a world beyond the mundane, spiritually uplifting works. 'Grotesque' covered dances that were dramatic, odd, funny and made people uncomfortable, curious, amused, flabbergasted. In putting each programme together a mixture of these experiences was offered.

To maintain a creative output sufficient to satisfy regular diversity was beyond the choreographic capacity of Laban and Bereska alone. The company, trained in any case as creative collaborators for works like *Der Schwingende Tempel*, also became choreographers producing solos and duos. These were used as additions to the basic repertoire created and performed by Laban, Bereska and the *Balletto Laban* dancers. To maximise on audiences returning again and again:

> ... familiar characters came into being, who were welcomed by the audience as old acquaintances just as in the medieval theatre. There were for example, the jester, the juggler, obstinacy, rage, playfulness, the dandy, the tyrant, death and many others.

On the matter of sound for the dances, which they managed themselves:

> Besides silent dances we performed works to the accompaniment of gong, drum and flute, or to simple music. All our music was composed expressly for our dances; existing music was really only used for folk dance.

They experimented with costume, partly for economy and partly to be able to perform the same movement material for a different effect.

> In our choice of décor and costume we still wavered between a stylisation of historical and theatrical forms on the one hand and the new characteristic style of our simple dance dress on the other. We even performed the same dances in different costumes, sometimes in a historical and at others in a timeless way so that we would not simply be guided by our own taste but also by reactions of the audiences, whom after all we wanted to attract in the first place.

As for movement material, while much of it came from his typical method of intention or task producing improvised movement, formed through bodily, choreutic and eukinetic articulation, he expanded the methods:

> We sometimes tried incorporating very simple movements and even everyday gestures into our dances. Some plays were built up out of affirmative nods, negative shakings of the head, defensive movements of the hands, beckoning waves, arms opening in surprise and similar everyday movements.

Klub der Sonderlinge (Club of the Eccentrics), a section in *Green Clowns*, is one such group piece, first danced as a quartet and *? ! (Interpunktionstanz)* (*? !* Punctuation Dance) one of Bereska's comedies. **4.4**

As well as solos and duos Laban and the company performed longer, usually amusing, works. He mentions particularly *Drachentöterie* (The Dragon Slayer), a fairy tale for a prince, princess and dragon, and the revival of the more ambitious *Oben und Unten* (Above and Below) also called *Himmel und Erde* (Heaven and Earth), first danced in 1921. **4.5**. The latter I recreated in the late 1980s.

> … it opened with a divided stage showing the starlit sky above and the stargazers below. With meticulous angular movements they execute their measurings and observations… their patience is rewarded for on the upper stage appear the evening star and two comets followed by many other stars and eventually the moon in person.

There follows an interaction as the astronomers fall in love with their adored objects and you can imagine the mayhem that could follow with at least one earnest stargazer taken up to heaven and comets falling to earth. The atmosphere of creative freedom that the 'Kammertanzers' enjoyed is caught in Laban's writing. They had nothing, so had nothing to lose and could allow their imagination and poverty of resources to produce a spontaneity that seems to have been passed on to their loyal spectators. Of rehearsals of *Oben und Unten* he wrote:

> Our leading lady [Bereska] who performed the moon was dancing with such elan
> and expression that all the members of the cast spontaneously hummed and
> whistled a melody which became the accompaniment.

Friedrich Wilckens, their composer/pianist when they could afford him,
would pick up their melody and improvise with it as the drama played out,[2]
or they would accompany it themselves with voice and percussion and any
melodic instrument that one of them had to hand.

Marsch (March) was a satirical quartet for four dancers with contrasting
body types. In my recreation the cast included one slender very tall young
man, one unusually short woman and two fairly robust women. **4.6** The
dance uses military parade movements seen in the quad marching, stamping,
turning, shuffling side-ways, many in unison but facing different directions.
Its comedy lay in the discrepancies caused by their unequal bodies and in
the gradual development of each as a character in the moments when they
are 'at ease'. The satirical element is given by the introduction towards the
conclusion of the Nazi marching style, the 'goose step'. The accompaniment
was a drumbeat and a penny whistle. It can be very funny indeed.

Looking at the archival records one can see that the *Kammertanzbühne*,
soon named Katabu, continued under Bereska's daily direction until she
left for Paris in 1929 when Laban took the post of Director of Movement
and Dance for the Prussian Theatres centred on the Berlin Opera at Unter
den Linden. Being Jewish she wisely did not follow Laban. The company
remained in Hamburg until 1926 when Laban opened the *Choreographisches
Institut* first in Wurzberg and then were centred in Berlin.

The company members also taught occasionally in the main school in
Hamburg and in the Institut and, when needed, in the other Laban schools
that opened all over German-speaking Europe, many with a Movement
Choir attached to them, fitting these in between performing with Laban in
major works such as *Don Juan* or *Gaukelei* and *Nacht*. To survive financially
they had to do what most dancers do today, perform whenever the
opportunity arose, give workshops, take class, choreograph, administer.
Some of the early members moved on, most to city opera companies or to
open their own schools. In 1928 when Laban had ceased performing and
was fully busy with the notation, the Institut, the Congresses, writing,
choreographing movement choirs, lecturing et al, the company became

---

2 Evelyn Dörr's reference to the work in her Appendix is misleading where she writes
'Dance theatre piece after music by Friedrich Wilckens and with German lyrics – folk song
like "Guter Mond, du geht so stille" (Good moon you move so quietly)'. The suggestion
here is that Wilckens wrote a score with sung folk song in it as a starting point for the
dance which is in absolute contrast to what occurred.

Kammertanzbühne Dussia Bereska and toured widely.[3]

Recreation of *Kammertanz Solos and Duos* 2012

I chose to focus on one group of solos and duos that would have premiered in performances during 1924/25 season rather than attempting dances from anywhere in the repertoire between 1923 and 1929. I was unable to find out enough about many of the copious number of pieces perhaps because they had a short life. Laban embraced the ephemerality of dances, they disappear as they are being performed unless considerable effortful rehearsal is undertaken to fix their form. What seems to have been the pattern was that programmes were put together for the zoo theatre and short tours with whomever was available making sure that the spectators would be offered a diverse experience through grotesque, ornamental, ecstatic and folk dances. The seven dances that I have selected offer the diversity Laban promoted when danced as a suite.

The research for these seven was undertaken in the late 1980s as were the first sketches and performances. The 2012 recreations were for camera for which dance filmmaker Roswitha Chesher was brought in. Robert Coleridge agreed to provide sound and Alison Curtis-Jones to support me with auditions and a second eye. The Studio Theatre at Trinity Laban was the venue, the production department providing technical support for lighting.

Mondäne (Chic) a solo for a man. The most significant information for this solo came from the choreographer Aurel Milloss.

Although Hungarian by birth he had spent much of his career in Germany and Italy, finally settling as a renowned figure in Rome. It was there that I located him and where he shared his experience of witnessing the *Kammertanzbühne Laban* on tour in Konstanz when he was a young ballet dancer. It so impressed him that he enrolled in the *Choreographisches Institut* when it opened in Berlin. He spoke and he demonstrated as best he could at a very considerable age.

Milloss recalled that Laban had danced *Mondäne* dressed in a dinner jacket, to a tango. It is the dance of a celebrity, a chic figure somewhat tired of it all. The Spanish flavour of the tango is picked up by suggestions of a matador in his body carriage, focus and arms and occasionally, in his feet, suggesting a bull, just mere suggestions. The dancer has to get a balance between the arrogance of himself, the celebrity status of both himself and the bull and the fatigue of having to keep the public, his public, engaged. The steps come loosely from the tango and the bullring.

3 The administrative papers of their tours, accounts and audience responses are available for study in the Tanzarchiv housed in Leipzig University Library.

The piece is highly dependent on the dancer whose interpretation can shift it more in one direction than another. For our first recreation in 1987 I collaborated with Dorothy Madden who, after discussing what had to be put in place, undertook the rehearsal direction with experienced performer Stuart Hopps. **4.7** I had invited Hopps because not only was he familiar with expressionist theatre but he was nearer the artistic maturity that Laban would have had than a young dancer. In 2012 I started with the form of the Madden/Hopps choreography, returned to what Milloss had indicated, and cast Macej Kuzminski, a Polish dancer with experience and strength of character. **4.8** His interpretation of almost the same steps as Hopps, emphasised the arrogance against which the nuances of weakness and suggestions of submission and boredom spoke well while Hopps had emphasised the tiredness of it all with memories of celebrity.

What the tango music was in Konstanz I have no way of knowing. Was it improvised? Was it well known? For this recreation I have gone to the composer/performer and accompanist that Laban had known in Germany and with whom he worked again in England, Adda Heynssen. She wrote two tangos, one more flamboyant than the other. I went for the more subtle sound so that the dancer could bring out the flamboyant moments of the movement himself and the nuances of the dance would not be swamped.

Krystall (The Crystal) a solo or duo for women.
Laban's autobiography mentions *Krystall* as one of his ornamental dances, an abstract dance, its theme being

> a feeling for form, a delight in line which divided space in hard, severe lines.

I believe that it was originally danced by Gertrud Snell who also danced *Ikosaeder*, Snell being his assistant for space studies and notation. **4.9, 4.10** Both of them are dances based on Laban's space harmony rings and scales. These are movement pathways, or trace forms as he calls them, in and around the crystal scaffolding of an icosahedron. In the case of *Krystall* the form used is an Axis Scale, an angular form balancing advancing with retreating, opening with crossing, rising with lowering, in six contrasting movements. **4.11** Just as a crystal has sharp faces and edges the dance has forms projecting into space quite sharply delineated.

The cast for this recreation was Verena Schneider and Ema Jancovic, graduates of Trinity Laban Conservatoire. Both had the technical facility required and a feeling for spatial form and the possibility that they could 'delight in line'. I could have decided to mount it as a solo but the second figure added interest especially in the second half of the dance. *Krystall*, because it has no references or narrative, can be dull. It has to satisfy the audience by its sheer beauty. Here we had two sensitive, articulate and confident dancers whose improvisation in the second half, where they 'delight' in the lines they draw in the space between them, carried the day.

For costumes silver was the right colour on glossy fabric to catch the shine of a crystal, and for the design I settled on the often worn cloche-like headgear, bra top and full pants. **4.12** This dance does not want a costume that emphasises 'womanly curves'. Snell was androgynous so I respected Laban's casting of her and played down the temptation to focus on the attractiveness of the dancers.

Robert Coleridge accompanied *Krystall* with metallic percussion, just filling the space delicately with vibration.

Marotte (Obsession) a solo for a man.

The dictionary gives the translation of marotte as 'quirky' but this is not the quality described by Aurel Milloss of Laban's performance in Konstanz. He said that Laban wore very little clothing, something like a loin cloth, that he was standing isolated in a spotlight and that the movement was organised as a rondo, A B A C A D A E and so on. To explain the A motif Milloss stood up and demonstrated a churning motion of his arm, fist over his navel, as if to mirror the inner churning of this unfortunate man. **4.13**

It is a grotesque expressionist movement piece, I would hardly call it a dance. The churning motif is strengthened by a look, the man knows he is being observed. The B motif is his obsession with cleanliness. The slapping of his hands and arms make a percussive sound, rhythmical jagged and uncontrolled. His churning motif returns and motif C develops from his audible breathing into a cacophony of laughing/crying. As in so many Expressionist pieces 'increase to crisis point' is the development method. Motif D is quiet, he drops to his knees and his hands feel the floor. What he does there is open to the performer, hitting, caressing, drawing... Back to the churning motif and on to Motif E which is violent, from imagined attackers he stumbles this way and that crying out as he defends himself. Caught again on the ever returning churning gesture the 'event' comes to an end with a complex motif built around the desire to comfort himself. **4.14** With Milloss's clear memory of the structure and look of the solos each recreation has a similarity of form.

Marotte is a disturbing piece to watch, and to rehearse and to perform. By no means all the men auditioning have managed it. To get at the expressionism he has to find a way of experiencing the state that the man is in and remove himself from the here and now into another world of madness, a perilous place in the land of silence. We cast Oliver Hornsby-Sayer. What helped him into the piece was his experience as a dancer in *Nacht*. There he had learnt from Curtis-Jones what expressionist grotesque demands in body, intention and voice.

He wears earth coloured male pants with a flap down the front, the costume style shown in many photographs of the male groups in the Laban circle. The sound comes entirely from the performer. The lit square in which he stands locates him as in a confined space.

I cannot be sure but I believe that this piece is the outcome of Laban observing the patients in the well-known asylum for the insane at Charenton-St Maurice, now in the suburbs of Paris, just down the road from where Laban was living with his first wife when a student of architecture at the Écoles des Beaux Arts.

Orchidée (The Orchid) a solo for a woman.
Orchidée was danced over several years always by Dussia Bereska. **4.15** The prime resource for the recreation was a short excerpt from the film *Wege zu Kraft und Schönheit* (The way to strength and beauty) made in 1924 on physical culture. In it Bereska is nude from the waist up while in the other photographs of it she is not. In my recreation I do include the nudity since there is ample evidence that dancing with no clothes was an occasional part of Laban's way of freeing his dancers from the constraints of bourgeois values. In the photographs of the Laban group at Monte Verita ten years earlier men and women are naked, Jenny Gertz children's and teenage boys' and girls' movement choirs are naked. Laban's *Choreographisches Institut* was ousted from Wurzberg in 1926 because of a nudity issue with his partner Gertrud Loeszer. **4.16** Gertrud Snell vouchsafed that nudity was not widespread in the *Kammertanzbühne* but occasionally, primarily for publicity, it was included.

Laban wrote that *Orchidée* was

> ... a solo by our leading lady which became well known and which was almost a symbol of the spirit of our theatre. It was called The Orchid, a composition of the most subtle arm and finger movements which got its name because it seemed to express the inner life of a bizarre flower in the process of unfolding.

The dance did not start as representative but as one in the ornamental abstract group. The idea of the orchid grew out of what Bereska was doing. In the 2012 recreation I started by using a peripheral 7-ring family as the trace form on which 'subtle arm and finger movements' can be developed, referring to but not aping the film fragment. I also use Laban's harmonic principle of the balance of opposites in that the movement is fundamentally curving and continuous with acceleration and deceleration and for balance I add moments of a quicker dropping bounce of her elbow, very small, suggesting drops of nectar.

Two dancers, Maeve Lamoliere and Chantelle Hicks, rehearsed the piece. **4.17** Bereska was seated on a dais in the film, closed in and down so we started there. The joy of working with Trinity Laban dancers is that they

4.1 Dussia Bereska, Director of the Kammertanzbühne Laban, 1924.

KAMMERTANZBÜHNE
RUDOLF VON LABAN

LEITUNG: DUSSIA BERESKA

4.2 Kammertanzbühne publicity material 1924/25.

REPERTOIRE
CHOREOGRAPHIE UND REGIE
RUDOLF V. LABAN U. DUSSIA BERESKA

Koltüme und Szenenbilder
nach Entwürfen Rudolf von Labans und Dussia Bereskas
Koltümatelier: Maria Diehl, Hamburg.

Ornamentale Tänze

1. Ballade . . . . Quartett
2. Kreuzgänge . . . . Frauengruppe
3. Isolaeder . . . . Gertrud Snell
4. Kryltall . . . . Dussia Bereska
5. Roletten . . . . Dussia Bereska
6. Zaubergarten . . Dussia Bereska, Rudolf von Laban, Motta Nolling
7. Orchidee . . . . Dussia Bereska
8. Arabesken . . . . Suite von Solis, Duos und Trios

Extatische Tänze
Byzanz:

9. Gebet . . . . Dussia Bereska, Rudolf von Laban
10. Molaik . . . . Dussia Bereska, Rudolf von Laban
11. Tempeltanz . . . Dussia Bereska, Rudolf von Laban Hermann Robst
12. Das Grauen . . . . Gruppe
13. Lustleid . . . Dussia Bereska, Rudolf von Laban
14. Der Mönch . . . . Rudolf von Laban
15. Schatten . . Rudolf von Laban, Hermann Robst
16. Träume . . . . Gruppe
17. Rituale und Opfertänze

Stiltänze
Alte Tanzvisionen:

18. Solo . . . . Dussia Bereska
19. Duo . . . . . Dussia Bereska, Hermann Robst
Bauerntänze:
20. Ungarische Motive
21. Slavische Motive
22. Romanische Motive
23. Schottische und deutsche Tänze
24. Chinesenstadt . . . . Hermann Robst

4.3 Kammertanzbühne Laban publicity material 1924/25.

Rhythmifche Tänze

25. Ipanema . . . . Rudolf von Laban
26. Ifriti . . . Rudolf von Laban, Hermann Roblt
27. Dithyrambus . Rudolf von Laban, Hermann Roblt
28. Marfch . . . . Quartett
29. Begegnung . . . Motta Nolling, Hermann Roblt
30. Troll . . . . Motta Nolling
31. Formate . . . . Rudolf von Laban
32. Rhythmifche Suite

Grotesktänze

33. Firlefanz . . . . Hermann Roblt
34. ?! (Interpunktionstanz) . . . . Dulfia Bereska
35. Marotte . . . . Rudolf von Laban
36. Mondänes . . . . Rudolf von Laban
37. Gruppengroteske
38. Klub der Sonderlinge . . . . . . Quartett
39. Irrwifche . . . . . Elfe Jüngling, Gretl Berner
40. Homunkulus . . . . . Rudolf von Laban
41. Phantaftifches Kabarett

Tanzfpiele

42. Drachentöterei, ein phantomimifcher Tanzfcherz
    Prinz . . . . . Dulfia Bereska
    Prinzeffin . . . Motta Nolling
    Drache . . . . Hermann Roblt

43. Terpfichore, ein Ballet von Händel
    Terpfichore . . . . Dulfia Bereska
    Faune und Nymphen

44. Das Idol, epifche Tanzfolge
45. Oben und unten, Tanzkomödie
46. Im Lande des Schweigens. Tanzfpiel

47. Don Juan, ein Tanzdrama
    Don Juan . . Rudolf von Laban
    Donna Elvira . . . Dulfia Bereska
    Spanarell ⎱ . . . Hermann Roblt
    Komthur ⎰
    Donna Anna . . Motta Nolling
    Volk. Gäfte und Dämonen

●

Die Nummern des heutigen Programms in der Beilage

4.3 continued

4.4 *Klub der Sonderlinge*
(Club of the Eccentrics),
Kammertanzbühne
Laban.

4.5 Drawing by Laban
of the Stargazers and
the Moon in *Oben und
Unten.*

4.6 Recreation of *Marsch* (March) 1991. Photographer Tony Nandi.

4.7 *Mondäne* (Chic). Stuart Hopps. 1987. Photographer Tony Nandi.

4.8 *Mondäne* Macej Kuzmunski 2013. Photograph Roswitha Chesher.

4.10 *Krystall*. Gertrud Snell 1924.
Photographer Wilm Burghaus.

4.9 *Krystall*. Gertrud Snell 1924.
Photographer Wilm Burghaus.

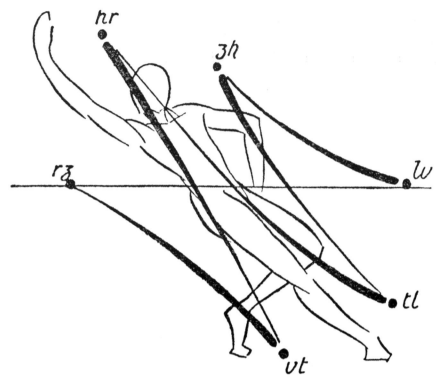

4.11 Diagram of the Axis scale. From Laban, R. *Choreographie* 1926.

4.12 *Krystall* 2013. Verena Schneider and Ema Jancovic. Photographer Roswitha Chesher.

4.13 *Marotte* (Obsessed) 1990. Photographer Tony Nandi.

4.14 *Marotte* 2013. Oliver Hornsby-Sayer. Photographer Roswitha Chesher.

4.15 *Orchidée* Dussia Bereska 1924. Photographer Anton Giulio Bagalia.

4.16 Gert Ruth Loeszer in a Kammertanz solo 1924. Photographer Alex Binder.

4.17 *Orchidée* 2013
Chantelle Hicks.

4.18 *Ekstatische* 1924.
Rudolf Laban and Othmar
Bartes.

4.19 Rudolf Laban in face mask in Wagner Duos 1925.

4.20 *Ekstatische* 2013. Oliver Hornsby-Sayer and Robert Keates.

4.21 Gert Ruth Loeszer in Kammertanz solo
1924. Photographer Alex Binder.

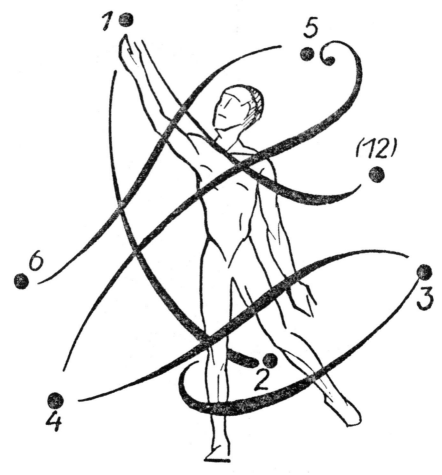

4.22 'A' Scale, the source of movement material in *Rosetten*.
From Laban, R. *Choreographie* 1926.

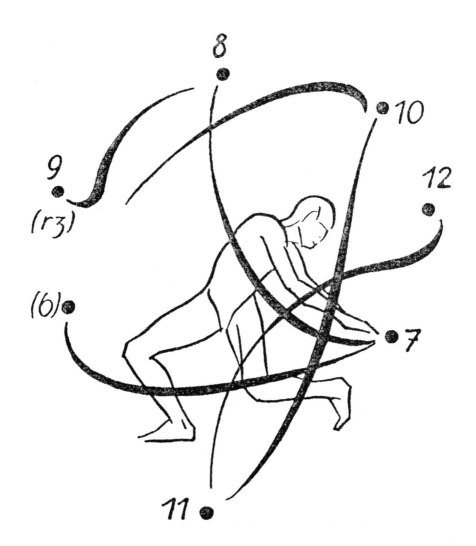

4.23 *Rosetten* 2013. Tara Saclier D'Arquian. Photographer Roswitha Chesher.

4.24 *Rosetten* 1990. Photographer
Toni Nandi.

4.25 Kurt Jooss while balletmaster at Munster 1925.

4.26 *Bizarre* 2013. Joel O'Donahue and Joshua Smith. Photographer Roswitha Chesher.

4.27 *Bizarre* 1990. Photographer Tony Nandi.

have the choreological language, as I guide them through 7 – 11 – 4 – 2 – 9, as a route of where their gestures will go, they know what I am taking about. These dancers had to discover subtlety of wrist and elbow; it is not a common demand from current choreographers.

For the audience naturally the nudity is an issue, it is what they tend to focus on. My job was in no way to make the dance salacious, it needs a coolness of performance with a distance between the spectator and the dancer that good lighting can assist. *Orchidée* is brief, it should be just a glimpse of the exotic.

Robert Coleridge enhanced the performance with an Indian bell, very delicate occasional sound. For the spectator, when these dances are performed as a suite, *Orchidée* is a perfect antidote to *Marotte*.

Ekstatische Zweimännertanz (Ecstatic dance for two men)
A photograph of Laban and Othmar Bartes wearing long straight gowns is the image that opens this priestly duo. **4.18** A strange masklike headdress completes the costume. In the image we have of it Laban is wearing the mask in one of the Wagner duos with Loeszer. **4.19** The dance has three sources, all of them coming from workshops on dance history given by Laban I attended as a student. Although he never referred to this dance by name, what he taught was 'ecstatic' movement material from ancient Egyptian ritual, then the Orthodox church ritual of his childhood, and the circling and whirling of the Mevlevi Dervishes that he witnessed in 'Constantinople' (Istanbul) and Herzegovina.

The Egyptian material uses the hard lines of the tetrahedron, the four-sided pyramidal structure, the first of the Platonic solids that, according to Laban's Rosicrucian studies, was/is the crystal of ecstasy. It certainly pulls the body into extreme attitudes of obeisance and adoration. Two men, Robert Keates and Oliver Hornsby-Sayer, were cast for this recreation. In an earlier mounting I had cast two mature men who added a priestly gravitas that the younger men had to work hard to match.

The Christian Orthodox material is a canon of consecration, the vibration of sacred energy, prostration, and receiving the spirit in head and heart. **4.20** The Dervish running, low with bent knees, flatfooted, leads into whirling, the palms cupped, one up one down, the dancer suspended between heaven and earth.

A deep gong vibrating through the space adds a soundscape. Ideally this dance should be performed at Stonehenge or in the stone circle on Harris in the Hebrides and that is certainly where I ask the dancers to locate their land of silence.

Rosetten (The Rose) a solo for a woman.

My understanding of this dance is that it is one of the very few dances that he made specifically to have an erotic layer masked in an apparently innocuous dance about a rose. It was danced by both his lovers of the period, Bereska and Gertrud Loeszer. **4.21**

The movement material is based on the A scale, his most well-known space harmony scale of twelve movements. The A and B scales are said by him to be complementary feminine and masculine scales respectively, according to the submitting or attacking nature of the axis around which the scale winds its pathways. The quality of the scale is heightened if, on the female /male continuum, the curves are emphasised in the A scale or the angles are emphasised in the B scale. **4.22** The material for *Rosetten* is a curvaceous performance of A scale movements choreographed in two short sections. **4.23, 4.24** In the first the dancer performs the movement close to her body so that it appears to be derived from behavioural gestures. In the second half she expands embracing the space around her. Throughout she is aware of her audience, looking at them eye to eye, presenting her femininity.

I rehearsed two dancers, Tara Saclier D'Arquian and Claire Lambert. For contemporary trained dancers for whom a non-gendered performance is the norm, the challenge lay in releasing the necessary eroticism for an expressionist dance. Both dancers had performed in *Nacht* where thoroughly 'depraved' performances were required in the *Tanzbar* scene. In *Rosetten* the sexuality is overt but subtle. The costume comes from a mix of two sources, a dress worn by Loeszer when she was partnering Laban in a Duo Tour in 1925, and the description Laban gives of the Queen of the Night in his autobiography, the first woman who showed him how feminine wiles functioned in Parisian high society. The 'Rose' wears a gown in deep red with white, elbow-length gloves and a red rose in her hair.

The music is the piano piece Slow Valse by Adda Heynssen.

Bizarre Zweimännertanz (A bizarre male duo)

This is a knockabout piece designed to end the show and send the audience home with a laugh. The costume sets the scene. The two men are bare-chested and wearing grass skirts, one of them sporting a pair of spectacles. The sources for *Bizarre* are a brief film of Kurt Jooss as a *Kammertanzer*. He is flapping his arms in what appears to be a fruitless attempt to take flight and whirling on the spot in pointless activity. In the film he is dressed in dark bloomers but in another photograph he wears the grass skirt. **4.25** Laban was known for his sense of humour. He drew sharp caricatures and entertained his dancers with hilarious mime.

The clue for the comedy is the bird. The opening dancer has to find a carriage of head and torso that makes clear his arrogant self-assurance. The image given to him to work with is of a young cockerel, cock of the roost, parading himself round his patch. When a similar figure, without glasses, enters and follows suit, a play on male competitiveness commences. **4.27**

The material is simple, prancing, arm flapping, foot slapping, elegant jumps, rustling of grass skirts. **4.26** Question and answer is the rhythm and subtle timing the art. Eventually they confront, the second figure shows off with fancy dance steps, whatever he is particularly skilled in, tap or Irish step dance et al, until the brooding 'cockerel' knocks him out and eventually hops on his back and is ridden away, preening.

I cast two Trinity Laban graduates, Joel O'Donahue and Joshua Smith. The sound comes from the dancers, padding and slapping feet, rustling skirts and a loud off-stage clap for the unexpected knock out slap.

These Dances are usually performed as Suite '24 in the order described here but that is my preference. Another order could suffice but this seems to provide the audience with a mix that has enough surprises in it to hold attention and end with a laugh.

Chapter Five
Recreating *Nacht* 1927
to *Night* 2010

The recreation of *Nacht* was a collaboration between myself and Alison Curtis-Jones. She was thoroughly acquainted with Laban's way of working having performed in my productions of *Die Grünen Clowns* (Green Clowns) and been responsible for its recreation in 2008 and 2009. I assembled the archives and together we sifted, discussed, studied, and suggested what the parameters for her studio realisation might be. The following are some of the issues we considered in terms of their impact on her practice.

Nacht was performed at the First Dancers' Congress held in Magdeburg, one of three evening-long works choreographed by Laban and performed over that weekend.**5.1**

The first presentation was *Titan*, a large choric work for amateur movement choirs. Of *Titan* Laban wrote:

> *Titan* was to show the power of community that I saw lying dormant in people. The base idea of this work was decidedly choric but at first I produced it with professional dancers. I visualised the spirit of community like a giant, a Titan who can and will break all fetters, and open up all the springs of humanity.[1]

Titan is a work that embodies his deeply felt values of the place of shared festive occasions in human wellbeing,

> The great festivals in life as well as the daily festive moments should be filled with a spiritual attitude which should concentrate on deepening the sense of mutuality and the appreciation of the personal identity of each individual.[2]

This sentence, written in 1935, was a way of stating to his Nazi employers his credo about people as valued individuals and on 'mutuality' as a mode of collaboration and not conformity. This credo was embodied in all his works in the way he valued a collaborative method and a respect for his contributing dancers as a community. The recreator of *Nacht* needs to embody the rotten values of *Nacht's* subject matter while employing a *Titan* method of mutuality towards the dancers.

> A genuine belief in the power of unity, in an unspoilt core within the human being gave me the inspiration for a dance-play, telling of the strength of the common hope which lies in a common will to achieve something better. This is *The Titan*.[3]

---

1 Titan was notated the following year and was the first dance to be remounted from the score, by Albrecht Knust.

2 Laban, 1935. p.84.

3 Laban, 1935. p.136.

Titan's reception at the Congress was mixed, as one would expect from the stratified dance public attending it. The movement choir members gathered were delighted by it, the rest were not, being opera ballet dancers and teachers, and Wigman and Schlemmer followers. The critics from the Theatre Exhibition had probably never seen such a work before and would have had no idea how to look at a participatory work. When *Titan* was reworked for the Busch Circus arena in Hamburg, with an enlarged cast and an audience of three thousand spectators, all amateur dancers, not surprisingly the performance, ninety minutes long, received a tumultuous response.

Ritterballett (Ballet of the Knights) was the third to be performed, a work commissioned by the spa town Bad Mergentheim where Beethoven had written a score of the same name.**5.2** A story of knights, their ladies, and court activities it was traditional in having an existing orchestral score. For the second evening Laban presented *Nacht*, not calling it a dance but a 'dynamic materialisation'. He saw these three performances as connected.

> In the *Ballet of the Knights* the past is caught, in *The Night* the present of that time and in *Titan* I saw the promise of the future.[4]

Each work would have had distinct resonances, both for and against, for the assembled dancer-based audiences. *Ritterballett* included:

> A hunt and a tournament, a pagan peasant rebellion, nuns defending the new and sacred belief in transcendental love, pages and country lasses secretly dancing together... a whirling train of gruesome and enchanting fairy-tale figures... with black storm banners of the ghostly knights.[5]

One can imagine the supporters of Schlemmer and Wigman finding this a facile theme while in general it 'aroused great delight everywhere' as the reviews corroborate.

Between these two *Nacht* was performed. **5.3, 5.4** Given that *Nacht* was a collaborative work what was Laban's own part in its creation? Firstly he was not dancing in it as he was in repertoire up to this time. His performing career almost ended in 1926 with a catastrophic event in the last scene of *Don Juan*:

> At its most dramatic finale Laban leapt off the raised stage as usual into 'hellfire' but no mattresses were in place to cushion his fall. He hit the ground hard, seriously injuring himself.[6]

He had two rehearsal assistants, Ruth Loeszer, a long-standing associate with whom he toured in 1925 with an audacious duo progranmme on Wagner characters, and Elinor Warsitz, who also performed in the work.

4 Laban, 1935, p. 181.
5 Laban, 1935, p. 183
6 Preston-Dunlop, 1998 ibid, p123.

It was Warsitz who wrote the detailed rehearsal notes that we were able to access.

Describes as 'out of the cycle *Die Erde* (The Earth)' *Nacht* refers back to the last section of his mammoth work on the The Animal, The Plant, The Crystal and Man planned in his youth but never realized in full.[7] He was supervising *Titan* (rehearsed by Margot Koch) and *Ritterballett* (rehearsed by Dussia Bereska) at the same time as creating *Nacht*. He was also using the gathering at the Congress to make the final difficult decisions on his notation. His close group, Kurt Jooss, with his collaborator from Munster Sigurd Leeder, Bereska and Gertrud Snell, plus Fritz Klingenbeck as scribe, were all there as he made the final alterations and decided to go public with the system at the next Congress. He had recently opened the *Choreographisches Institut* in Wurzberg and was masterminding the Congress. Although the man was a polymath by nature a great many all-absorbing activities were going on simultaneously.

Of *Nacht* he wrote:

> The play opened with a crown of mechanically grinning society men and women, followed by all I had experienced and felt when I first met life in the big city. It was built around a fantasy on work which showed money being earned without work. Greed, covetousness, adoration of three idols: dollars, deceit and depravity. The whole wild orgy found no solution and ended in madness.[8]

The chapter entitled The Night in his autobiography describes his experiences in Paris when he was taken under the wing of a wealthy socialite he called The Queen of the Night. Elegant, alluring, she sat centre stage in her salon surrounded by pretentious pseudo poets vying for her attention. She introduced the inexperienced youth that Laban was to all the pleasures of the wealthy in a decadent city. Hence, 'dollars, deceit and depravity' being the topics of *Nacht*. The salon became the starting point for scene one in our 2010 recreation, the gambling and stockbroking greed for scene two, the drink, drugs and sex for scene three.

> How can true beauty dwell among the glitter of tattered silk and under the artificial purple lights? How can the soul rejoice amid the rags of the poor and the hollow eyes of hungry children? How utterly remote is the fragrance of the mountain and forests from the air of the slums, so thick with coal dust and the deadly smell of the powdered prostitute! Is this the song of man?[9]

What became scene four concentrated on the poverty, dirt and unrelenting labour that lay hidden beneath the veneer of respectability that the 'shop girl', the 'waiter', or any underpaid minion suffered. It was the juxtaposition

7 Lisa Ullman, Diana Jordan and Sylvia Bodmer directed a performance of *The Earth*, a free interpretation of the original sketches in a Summer School in 1959.
8 Laban, 1935, p.45.
9 Laban, 1935, p.43.

of the dollars-driven depravity of the rich with the deceitful cover up of the distress of the poor who serviced their fun that got to him.

His words refer to *fin de siècle* Paris, while *Nacht* is placed in the quagmire of Weimar Germany. George Grosz's well-known cartoons capture bloated profiteers leering at prostitutes, beside middleclass bourgoisie, beside the decrepit condition of war wounded and the suffering of the workless masses. Particular to Weimar Germany was the deceit. The nation was suffering shattered pride from losing the war and fury at the overblown reparations demanded by the victors. The people were knocked sideways by financial ruin and political chaos. By 1933 the tension will erupt under Hitler but in the 1920s it smouldered as people lived it up to hide their true feelings, with morality tested on any front you care to mention.

Laban was aware that other choreographers, filmmakers and playwrights had dealt with the same scenario:

> What the revues and the films of our day made out to be charming and chic, sophisticated and smart, what people took for terribly sweet and amusing, I portrayed here with its true bitter aftertaste, with its obnoxious flavour and its degrading nastiness.[10]

The critics stated there was no let-up in the onslaught on the audience, including from the music that was 'a critique of jazz'. *Nacht* was too strong. The evening-long performance was greeted with '*Turbulenz mit Pfiffen und Applaus*' the audience on their feet, whistling with loud hand clapping.[11] It was, as Laban judged at that moment, 'an absolute flop', a flop for that audience at the 1927 Dancers' Congress. Years later he vouchsafed that he thought it was one of his strongest statements and for that reason I looked at it as a possible work to recreate. One critic wrote

> Why I ask myself do not all dances have such inner strength as is expressed in Laban's productions?[12]

Another stated that if the performance had been condensed into a much shorter work it had a sharp statement to make. That is what Curtis-Jones and I agreed to do, cutting down thirteen scenes to four and attempting to make 'a sharp statement' with 'inner strength'. Five years later Kurt Jooss would pick up the theme of *Nacht* in his ballet *The Big City*. He certainly did not make it charming and chic but nor did he give it the full frontal Expressionist punch that Curtis-Jones, and the dancers had to achieve in the recreation of *Nacht* and did.

The image that gave *Nacht* its visual flavour came from the *Tanzarchiv*

10 Laban, 1935, p.43.
11 Loesch, I. *Mit Leib und Seele: Erlebte Vergangenheit des Ausdrucktanzrs*. Berlin: Henschelverlag, p.67.
12 S. Ebg. Dance Performance 1927 in unidentified newspaper cutting signed S Ebg.

in Leipzig, sharp designs for the head and face of various archetypal characters. **5.6 , 5.7** We focused on the top-hatted, monocled man, a wide-eyed smooth-haired girl and a turbaned sunken-eyed woman. For its sonic flavour we listened to 1920s jazz and Berlin Cabaret music and engaged Oli Newman, a Trinity Laban musician, with the responsibility to provide what a 'caricature of jazz' might have amounted to in 1927 and how it might sound in 2010. We studied the images of Kark Hubbuch, Heinrich Ehmsen and Jeanne Mammen to build up a sense of the distress of the times.

The prime archive is the rehearsal script written by Elinor Warsitz. One could reconstruct movement phrases from it and pathways but for us it had a serious drawback. It was unclear which of the thirteen scenes the description referred to nor was there any indication of the intention of the 'three steps' or 'turn left' which for an Expressionist work was essential to know. What it did give us was a sense of the detail, the kind of movement, the male/female relationships, rhythms and floor plans. *Monotonie* was a title that kept returning. From the drawing of a tableau in his autobiography he had figures of poverty as well as top-hatted bankers. **5.5** We contemplated including both but realised that we would have to deal with more scenes than were possible within the constraints of time and budget to do so. It is in the last scene, which we entitled *Monotony*, that labour and worklessness is the topic. Jooss was more explicit in *Big City* with a mother in a shawl and two barefoot children, but we went for the inner stirrings of distress in general.

Unlike *Green Clowns* the various scenes had no titles in the original programme. We could have played the recreation as continuous but decided that scene titles would help everyone. Scene One, 'Smart Set' is not a Laban phrase but the translated title of the lyrics of a cabaret song of the period. It recalls the wannabe smart young men surrounding the Queen of the Night, so that is what we decided upon. 'Stockbrokers' is the title we gave to the gambling scene, lifted directly from Laban's writing but in the next recreation of *Nacht* I may use 'Dollars'. 'Tanzbar' comes from the title of a sketch by Jeanne Mammen drawn in 1927 in which she forefronts a same-sex couple.

With this background in place Alison Curtis-Jones started the studio work.

From Archive to Production
Alison Curtis-Jones with Oli Newman

Nacht's portrayal of Weimar Germany is highly topical and contemporary; resonating with today's current economic climate of banking crises, global recession, political corruption and toxic celebrity culture. London 2010 provided a fitting context for the dancers to encounter the thrust of *Nacht's* pertinent issues.

My role as recreator, was to examine archive evidence with Dr Valerie Preston-Dunlop, to investigate the cultural context of the Weimar period and function in the studio as creator/facilitator of movement and director of dancers' responses.

With little evidence of the original surface form of *Nacht* an exact exhumation is impossible.[13] My intention was not to create a contemporary interpretation of the work, but to use archeochoreological methods[14] to draw as closely as possible from the sources available and engage with them to operate Laban's known approaches to dance theatre practice during the studio research stages.

My dialogue was with documents, pictures, programme notes et al and not with the work itself. How, with these limited resources, could I create the movement material to resemble a piece I had never witnessed? Dr Leslie-Anne Sayers states:

> At issue here is not the simple case of one work being inspired by an earlier one, but the more complex one in which a new work emerges from a close analysis and creative dialogue with an earlier work and its contexts.[15]

In my previous experiences of recreating Laban's *Die Grünen Clowns* in 2008, 2009 for Trinity Laban dancers and again in 2008 for Transitions Dance Company[16], I had benefitted from the research Preston-Dunlop had already undertaken over a number of years to establish the sequence of events in the work. The experience gave me considerable insight and practical knowledge of Laban's approaches and methodologies. In recreating *Die Grünen Clowns* in 2008, I was re-working a draft of *Green Clowns* already in place. With *Nacht*, I was starting from pieces of paper. I had to organise the sequence of events and create a legitimate work so that *Night 2010* could be valued not only as a dance theatre work in its own right, but as a valid historical insight into 1927's *Nacht* and Laban's Dance Theatre repertoire. Preston-Dunlop writes:

> Recreation of any sort begs the question: is the new production sufficiently imbued with the originator's style to warrant his or her name being attached to it?[17]

13 Millicent Hodson, choreographer and dance historian – internationally recognised for her reconstructions of early 20th Century Ballets including *Le Sacre du Printemps*, discusses issues of authenticity with collaborator Kenneth Archer in 'Confronting Oblivion, Preservation Politics, 1.
14 Methods used to 'find' lost dances. *Dance Chronicle*, 2011, p.5.
15 *Dance Chronicle*, 2011, p.30.
16 Transitions Dance Company performed my recreation of *Green Clowns* at Dartington Hall and in Manchester as part of the celebrations marking 50 years after Laban's death.
17 *Dance Chronicle*, 2011, p.23.

In bringing the work out of the archive into the theatre, the dilemma of staying true to what Laban was trying to say meant I had to balance my own artistic approach with a Laban Expressionist stamp firmly embedded in the process.

> All living art draws its nourishment from the atmosphere of the time from whence it comes.[18]

This new *Nacht* would be nourished by the contributions made by the dancers in 2010, their (and my) life experiences and training programmes, a world apart from those of the original Kammertanzers and Laban himself.[19]

My practical research for *Night 2010* began with a group of Trinity Laban alumni in 2009. These dancers had experienced my working practices through collaborating with me to recreate *Green Clowns* in 2008 and 2009. Their contribution was invaluable. I was able to experiment with specific ideas in the studio. Transferring ideas into practice proved to be a challenging investigation. Ideas in principle, generated from studying the sources, did not always work in practice.

The process of recreating an Expressionist dance theatre work, demanded a different way of working for my 2010 dancers. Expressivity has to be achieved from a deeply felt experience, dancers must have intention, to feel sensations first, then with my help, shape the form using choreutic and eukinetic principles. Dance Expressionism is not mime or acting, nor is it adding an expression to an already defined movement, it is a feeling imbuing the entire body. The characterisation comes through an integration of feeling, intending, doing, corporeally.

Laban's approach to process; the use of improvisation and of drawing movement contributions from dancers, is used extensively in today's choreographic practice. What I found interesting when I started work with the cast, was that improvisation tasks that I carefully structured to produce particular images from the 1920s presented difficulties, because dancers today move with a concern either for abstraction or with strong somatic practices in their training. Expressionist movement responses proved difficult. I did not want to dismiss the dancers' contributions, far from it, but I had to deal with the training practices of these current dance artists to enable the needs of the work I was recreating to emerge. These dancers are also not the mature men and women that Laban worked with in 1927, they

---

18 Preston-Dunlop, V. and Lahusen, S. *Schrifttanz*.1990, p.7.

19 My own dance practice and pedagogy has developed through practical engagement with Laban's principles and through teaching Choreological Studies at Trinity Laban Conservatoire for Music and Dance and that expertise was directly pertinent to *Nacht*. But alongside was my independent choreographic practice and teaching of contemporary technique. My own choreographic aesthetic and the technique had to be re-organised to prepare the dancers for Expressionism.

are dance artists in training, albeit, sophisticated, skilled and inquisitive, they are still, however, honing their technical and creative and performance skills. I challenged them to be corporeally daring, to break out of the safe haven of the known.

To facilitate the movement for the recreations, I taught supporting contemporary technique classes informed by Laban principles. These classes were designed not only to develop the dancers' technical skills but also to introduce a 1920s style of moving and to expand the way they embodied material. The classes also deepened their skills in choreutic and eukinetic principles through using choreological language, a common terminology for movement principles. As there is no 'codified' 'Laban technique', I had to research the possibilities of establishing a movement base relevant to the work and to challenge the technical proficiency of the dancers. I made it clear to them that this process was not about them dancing like 1920s dancers, they are 2010 dancers and we could not ignore this fact. Preston-Dunlop passed on movements from her own time of working with Laban and from Sylvia Bodmer who was in Laban's group in 1921.[20]

My approach to technique is physically demanding. It includes dancing spatial scales and rings, using the kinesphere, lability, harmonic opposition, developing the dancer's spatial awareness and understanding of choreutic form. With complex rhythmic material the class demands a wide dynamic range and use of effort qualities. I also include distinct choreutic perspective, using 'swings' in the vertical, horizontal and sagittal planes, working with and from 'centre',

> ...concern with the centre of energy resonates with the Rosicrucian practice of locating and sensitising centres both within and outside the body.[21]

gathering and scattering, exploring figure-of-eight forms, the lemniscate, three dimensional cross and icosahedral orientation.

The technical base consists of congruent body co-ordination, with intense commitment to the movement, deeply felt performance and a high level of group sensitivity. During these classes, I developed their ability to occupy the space, to be present in the space, awareness of three dimensionality of the body and of engaging with 'the body in space' as well as 'space in the body', density of space, their intention in ChU/Mm, not just as designs and shapes in space, but how it is to feel these choreutic choices.[22] We worked on stillness and how to work physically and emotionally to keep stillness

---

20 There is video footage of some of these exercises by Sylvia Bodmer entitled *'In the Laban Tradition'*. 1986. Available in The Laban Collection.

21 Preston-Dunlop, V. *Rudolf Laban, An Extraordinary Life*, 1998, p.11.

22 ChU/Mm – Choreutic Unit and Manner of Materialisation – creating actual and virtual lines and curves in the body and in space through body design, spatial progression, spatial projection and spatial tension. (Preston-Dunlop, V. *Looking at Dances*, 1998, p.133).

alive and allow it to resonate. We investigated specific locations in space, and William Forsythe's development of Laban's ideas to encourage acute understanding of spatial articulation. Forsythe's rupturing of Laban's choreutic laws, using 'superzoning' and crossing over the centre line of the body, and questioning where 'centre' might be, has created a new living architecture.

Forsythe's experimentation and questioning of Laban's structures highlights the responsibilities of artists to adhere to or to rupture the traditions they inherit. We had inherited the themes in *Nacht*, and we had to decide what we were going to adhere to and to rupture – this gave the dancers a responsibility to contribute to the process and therefore to change the form. Laban's way of working embraced rupture, if our process was to be a true reflection of his approach, then the form of *Nacht* will change with each mounting.

Preston-Dunlop and I selected four of the original thirteen sections, partly because the duration of the new *Nacht* was 25 minutes compared with Laban's whole evening, and partly because the archives were incomplete. Such an edited version was in any case called for by the press at the time. The critical response to *Nacht* in 1927 was hostile:

> a great ranting and raving of criticism, a fright for the public, in fact a diarrhoea like never before, an absolute debacle.[23]

Laban's 1927 opening sequence was entitled 'Queen of the Night' and we considered a number of ways to deal with this. Laban's marked distaste for the superficialities of high society spoke loudly in his writings, so we began with a section, to which we gave a working title *'Smart Set'*, to illustrate 1920s chic. Then followed *'Stockbrokers'*, *'Tanzbar'* and *'Monotony'*. Each section referred to Laban's three key themes *'Dollars, Depravity and Deceit.'*[24]

We worked with costume and music collaborators for the 2010 production. **5.8** Costume designer, Martina Trottman, was inspired by the original designs of Hans Blanke. Fay Patterson, lighting designer and Senior Technician at Trinity Laban, agreed to provide a nighttime atmosphere and sinister mood for the work. Composer and musician, Oli Newman took on the score. He writes:

> Unfortunately, the original music had been lost, as well as any reference to the original music, except for one margin note... My background is as a composer of contemporary music... I have no background in music history or musicology... In fact, I was encouraged to make something more modern. As an audience, we look at this snapshot from history knowing what happened next, we can't see it without knowing of a broader historical and artistic picture. So a modern score would sit well with this broader reading of the context.

23 Dörr, 2008, p.133.
24 Laban, 1935, p.45.

The sound was an integral part of the studio work and performance, Newman writes:

> Budget and space constraints meant a very small (music) ensemble. It was decided early on that we would perform live, on the stage, and the lineup would centre around piano and drums. I started work on four main pieces with a short interlude to transition between the second and third scenes.

Smart Set – Deceit

The movement in '*Smart Set*' explores the superficiality of social etiquette at the time, how people conduct themselves in social situations, the notion of high society, where appropriate behaviour and social acceptance dictate, much like the celebrity culture of today, where appearance is everything. **5.9**

I used 1920s photographs and images to inspire the dancers. The top hats made by Trottman from the Blanke costume designs became a useful prop, with dancers tipping the rim of the hat and changing its angle in relation to the body. White make up, a monocle and moustache were in the design, drawing immediate attention to facial expressions which we experimented with as a feature throughout the rehearsals. The women wore wide flared silk pants, with glittering tops and headdress over chic black bob wigs, with made up white faces, thick red lips, blue eye shadow with false lashes and thick black eyeliner. Liza Minelli in Fosse's *Cabaret* came to mind.

For movement to suggest intellectual, chic, smart glamour and polite society, I elicited small articulate gestures, bowing, clicking heels, formal greetings, stirring tea, holding a cigarette with head poised, and 'doing' it in the right 'fashion'. Gestures of preening, framed by postures, using choreutic chords were defined. Surfaces of the body moved into and out of specific spatial locations. I challenged the dancers to articulate precisely, with movement restricted within the kinesphere in 'mini zone' for 'the inner wretchedness of the wealthy'[25] and extending into the 'superzone',[26] for the 'outward veneer portraying artificial sophistication...' and to show the 'pathetic illusion of happiness' identified by Laban.[27] To make more of this material, I manipulated it using a variety of transformation techniques such as repetition and choreutic transposition, used more recently by choreographer Forsythe[28] and I ignored laws of sequentiality,

25 Laban, 1935, p.42.
26 Laban, *Choreutics*, 1966, p.23.
27 Laban, 1935, p.42.
28 Baudoin P., and Gilpin H. Proliferation and Perfect Disorder in Programme of Reggio Emilia William Forsythe Festival Danza, 1989.

by breaking the choreological order[29] to make movement inorganic, to create the 'ugliness' referred to in Laban's writings.[30] Research of Valeska Gert's use of the grotesque helped to inspire movement for 'Smart Set'.

> Valeska Gert did not shy away from realism, even if it meant dealing with the uglier aspects of human behaviour.[31]

I also studied photographs of Aurel Milloss, a former pupil and follower of Laban, whose expressivity at the time was distinctive. His dramatic temperament, his preference for the macabre and grotesque are visible in photographs of his solos.[32]

I gave the characters a sinister undertone through their facial expressions choreographed using harmonic opposition, decentralisation, location and pathways. The characters are not entirely trustworthy, their presentation of self, seen in 'outward' gestures of flicking and dabbing effort qualities. Dancers had to work with rigour to articulate the detail in the material, some gestures were small and subtle and had to be clearly defined to be seen by the audience.

> ... groups of people who were stirring their teacups with an air of profundity, their little fingers affectedly crooked.[33]

These lines from lyrics from a Berlin Cabaret song provided another source of inspiration for some of the movement ideas.

Cut off crusts
Cut off lusts
Minds a sieve

Kiss ladies hands
Brushing off dust

You want out

---

29 A movement makes sense only if it progresses organically and this means that phases which follow each other in natural succession must be chosen. It is therefore essential to find the natural characteristics of the single phases which we wish to join together in order to create a sensible sequence. (Laban, 1966, p.4).

We must try to find its (movement's) real structure and the choreological order within it through which movement becomes penetrable, meaningful and understandable. (ibid.p.viii).

30 Laban, 1935, p.41.

31 Schlee, in Preston-Dunlop, V. and Lahusen, S. Schrifttanz.1990, p.5

32 Images of Milloss in Tanz eines, 1928, p.6, Milloss in The Madman and Death, 1937, p.8, Milloss as the Miraculous Mandarin, 1942, p.14 in Photographs for Milloss, (Ed)Veroli, P. Jan 1999.

33 Laban, 1935. p 34.

Burn to shout
Inside itches

We flock together
Birds of a feather
Chat, nothing to say
Take on quiet topics

Shout 'Oh No!'

Shudder
Present a button hole
Smoke a cigarette
In a loignette [34]

In contrast to the '*Smart Set*' gestures we devised a sequence to contrast 'the outward veneer' and to illustrate the paradox in the lyrics. Dancers experimented with inward movement material, towards the body's centre, using a wringing effort quality. The movement was located in the gut and in the heart... where the pain is. This material was not set and would vary from one performance to the next, with dancers responding phenomenologically.

Elinor Warsitz's rehearsal notes were used to establish some of the floor plans. The notes did not specify to which sections of the dance the floor plans referred, but they gave a clear indication of the detailed use of space in the original. Laban stated 'The play opened with a crowd of mechanically grinning society men and women'.[35] and the first page of Warsitz's notes showed a semicircle. I used this for the opening image adding a catwalk linear pathway through the centre, as in the notes.

> The men around her (The Queen of the Night) competed in saying or doing something exceptional.[36]

Celebrities were shown, centre stage, surrounded by adoring fans, a semi circle of hand clapping, smirking observers, framing each soloist whose 'clever' footwork, performed with competitive edge, caught the eye. The characters positioned their clapping hands in locations of the icosahedron, using the sequential form of Laban's A Scale.[37]

---

34 See the song lyrics, 'It's All A Swindle', 'Sex Appeal' and 'The Smart Set' on Entartete Musik: Berlin Cabaret Songs, CD, Decca, 1997.
35 Laban, 1935, p.43.
36 Laban, 1935, p.32.
37 I drew from Laban's *Choreutics* 1966, written after *Nacht* was first created in 1927, but these principles and influences were significant in the recreation process.

The 'Women in Gold', the turbaned sunken-eyed characters,[38] are gross. Their loud, wide, strutting entrance breaks the illusion of chic – they are almost caricatures of themselves, and of today's artificial image of botox blown, bosom implanted horrors who have physically destroyed themselves in pursuit of 'perfection'. The 'Women in Gold' exaggerate their material through repetition and transformation techniques, pushing their gestures further into the extremes of space, mouths contorted further than is comfortable, lips pouting in the sagittal plane and tongues protruding in various spatial locations. Their presence in this section provides a critique of the social context and notion of 'beauty' or 'smart'. This image of pretence or 'deceit',[39] highlights Laban's sense of horror of the 1927 culture. During the performance the sound here is loud, crashing and beating its way into the auditorium – uncomfortable for the audience's eye and ear, a meleé of high class chic juxtaposed with the grotesque.

I rehearsed with Jazz music to help dancers locate the era – not setting movement specifically to the score initially, but these pieces of music were certainly influential in the stylisation of the material. I kept awareness of Laban's own music score, 'beat for beat in rhythm and metre from the pen of Laban'[40], in contrast to his well-documented approach of freeing movement from the constraints of music. My decision was to set a time signature against which dancers would articulate rhythmic patterns. We worked specifically with impulse, impact, rebound, swing and continuous,[41] with gestures performed over one or two bars, using the downbeat at the beginning of the bar as a significant point in the phrasing.

Musician Oli Newman, attended rehearsals to see the movement emerging. In true Laban tradition, the movement was not dictated to by the score, Newman's new score was composed to support the movement. Newman writes:

> The first section used elements of European jazz. I listened to several pieces by Django Reinhardt and decided that gypsy jazz would be an interesting addition to the mix of references. Also included are some Klezmer and Yiddish folk music ideas. The chord sequence for the guitar part at the end of the piece refers to the chords in the Tanzbar song.

In the performance, the characters emerge out of the darkness, in a semi circle. The live drumming is uncomfortably loud to ambush the audience, a clash of aesthetic image with thumping, crashing percussion.

---

38 Taken from images from the Tanzarchiv in Leipzig
39 Laban, 1935, p.45.
40 Erich Ytar Kahn wrote the music for *Nacht*, (1927) following Laban's notation of the rhythms and meters bar by bar. The conductor in Magdeburg was Rudolf Wagner-Regeny. (*A Life for Dance*, p.45)
41 Laban, R, *Choreographie.*

5.1   A poster for *Titan, Nacht* and *Ritterballett*, German Theatre Exhibition, Magdeburg, 1927.

Sonntag, den 19. Juni 1927, 7.30 Uhr abends

RITTERBALLETT

Tanzspiel nach historischen Motiven in vier Reigen von Rutholph Laban

Choreographie: Rutholph Laban

Musik: Ludwig van Beethoven mit eingefügten Musikstücken aus anderen Beethovenschen Balletten und stummen Szenen
Regie und Einstudierung: Dussia Bereska
Kostüme und Bühnengestaltung: Hans Blanke, Gera
Regieassistenz: Liesel Löser II
Dirigent: Rudolf Wagner-Régeny

Gestalten: 6 Ritter: 6 Ritterfräulein, 6 Nonnen, 6 Bauernmädchen:

6 Ritter:	6 Ritterfräulein, 6 Nonnen, 6 Bauernmädchen:
Roman Ihlen	Eva Ahlemann
Susanne Ivers	Irmgard Berve
Ilse Loesch	Hanna Wolff
Hermann Robst	Hildegard Liebermann
Ilse Schulz-Brummer	Irma Lutz
Will Schwarz	Gerda Rauh

6 Pagen:	6 Klopfgeister:	6 Bauern, 6 Jäger:
Ilse Boy	Ilse Graef	Ilse Berlitzheimer
Heinz Effner	Rose Mirelmann	Maxim Bosse
Erika Hillebrecht	Lisa Mutschelknaus	Irma Heinrichsdorff
Lola Rogge	Resi Regensteiner	Margarete Hornauer
Luci Wientz	Anni Sauer	Gerda Höller
Ruth Döring	Anni Weiß	Margot Koch

Der Großmeister . Heinz Landes · Die Hexe . Liesel Löser II

I. Reigen: Musikalisches Vorspiel
1. Tanz der Wilden und der Hexe. 2. Aufzug der Ritter. Bekehrung und Dankgebet.

II. Reigen: 1. Tanz der Klopfgeister, Pagen und Bauern. 2. Rondo der Ritterfräulein und Pagen. 3. Aufmarsch zum Fest.

III. Reigen: 1. Musikloses Vorspiel. 2. Bauernaufruhr. 3. Aufzug der heiligen Frauen. Ueberfall. 4. Befreiung durch die Ritter.

IV. Reigen: 1. Jägerlied. 2. Liebesspiel. 3. Gespensternacht. 4. Die schwarzen Scharen.

Ausführung der Kostüme unter Mitwirkung von Frl. Cilli Amber, Meisterschülerin des Choreographischen Instituts Laban.

SZENEN AUS „NACHT" UND „TITAN"

Große Pausen nach dem Ritterballett und den Szenen aus „Nacht"

5.2 Programme of *Ritterballett* at the First Dancers' Congress, 1927.

Sonnabend, den 18. Juni 1927, 8 Uhr abends

NACHT

Dynamische Materialisationen für große Gruppe in 13 Bildern und einem Musikvorspiel. Aus dem Zyklus „Die Erde" von Rutholph Laban

Motto: Was dem Menschen unbewußt . . . .
durch das Labyrinth der Brust
wandelt in der Nacht.   *Goethe*

Choreographie: R u t h o l p h   L a b a n

Tonkomposition: Erich Itor Kahn, Frankfurt
Regie und Einstudierung: Ruth Loescer
Kostüme und Bühnengestaltung: Hans Blanke, Gera
Regieassistenz: Elinor Warsitz
Dirigent: Rudolf Wagner-Régeny
Am Flügel: Der Komponist Erich Itor Kahn

Mitwirkende:

Die Damen:	Ursula Ackermann	Susanne Kaßbitz	Annemarie Sievers
	Rosi Anfänger	Eva Kreis	Elinor Warsitz
	Rosemarie Gerig	Thus Lang	Hanna Wolff
	Marie Hulkowa	Daisy Rensburg	

Die Herren:	Cilli Amber	Trude Einecke-Bosse	Hildegard Lipinski
	Benedikt Bervert	Ilse Halberstam	Gertrud Snell
	Hedwig Böckmann	Fritz Klingenbeck	Richard Thum
	Willi Borrmann	Julie Kolmer	

3 G ö t z e n b i l d e r * * *   u n d   w e i t e r e   4 0   T ä n z e r

Die Gestalten: Menschen des Alltags — Unserer Zeit — Zeitlos — Vereinigt in bunter Gesellschaft — Männer und Frauen verschiedener Welten — Kinder und Halbwüchsige — Vorbeiziehende „Leute" — Denker — Sportler — Zimmermädchen — Boys und Fanatiker

A u s f ü h r u n g   d e r   K o s t ü m e :   F r a u   v o n   C a r l o w i t z ,   D r e s d e n

G r o ß e   P a u s e   n a c h   d e m   5 .   B i l d

5.3 Programme of *Nacht* at the First Dancers' Congress, 1927.

5.4 Press call of *Nacht* 1927. Photographer Rudolf Hatzold.

5.5 Drawing by Laban: *Dance of the Greedy* from *Nacht*.

5.6 Headdress and mask design for *Nacht* 1927 by Hans Blanke.

5.7 Headdress and mask design for *Nacht* 1927 by Hans Blanke.

5.8 Costume designs for *Night 2010* by Martina Grossman.

5.9 *Nacht 2011 Smart Set*. Photographer Kyle Stevenson.

5.10 *Nacht 2010 Stockbrokers*. Photographer Kyle Stevenson.

5.11 *Nacht 2010 Tanzbar*. Photographer Kyle Stevenson.

5.12 *Nacht 2010 Monotony.* Photographer Kyle Stevenson.

The dancers exit, the sound diminishes, until they re-emerge, low level, into the toxic gambling den.

Stockbrokers – Dollars

This section deals with dollars, the hunger for making money at all costs. Greed and winning count for everything. 'Thieves kitchens and gambling dens'[42] are established through various close groupings in the general space. Stockbrokers, the stock exchange, frenetic buying and selling all provided images for movement. **5.10**

> I went to the stock exchange and watched the excited jobbers pushing and shoving in and out, with fixed stares on their faces, shouting hoarsely and brandishing bits of paper.[43]

The gestures of 'Tic Tac' men at the races, small, quick gestures of the hands and head, I placed in a demanding rhythmic structure, repeated at speed, to create a frenetic scene.

The toss of a coin became a significant moment, with dancers responding with a body design of despair or elation. The actions of tossing coins and throwing dice were defined using ChU/Mm, the toss of a coin performed with an impulse followed by an impact down, finishing in a body design. The throwing of dice was performed with a curved spatial progression in a peripheral pathway in the sagittal plane, ending with straight projection, to define the material.

The dancers' behaviour contrasts significantly with the previous section, '*Smart Set*'. There is much greater use of the general space and individuals moving across the space, and through the space, changing orientation and creating new group formations.

The material is fast, with images of dealing cards, grabbing money, of secrecy and hiding cards, aggressive pushing and shoving and jumping in desperation and for joy. Activities change quickly, with characters crowding around to see a roulette wheel. The section builds to a climax; the material is developed using change of orientation and spatial planes. The elation of winning is contrasted with moments of stillness where dancers hold body designs of either winning or losing, accompanied by a break in sound. The 'liveness' of this is evident in each performance, as timing varies in each case. Newman writes:

> The second section speeds up and takes a darker turn. The piano part is still rooted in jazz, but contains references to Schoenberg, Kurt Weill, Hans Eisler and Bernard Hermann. These composers were chosen in part because they had fled Europe in the 30s and 40s. Hermann, though born in New York, sounded very

42 Laban, 1935, p.38.
43 Laban, 1935, p.41.

European, and as his most famous works were in film scores, most often for Alfred Hitchcock, it was a very simple way to imbue the music with a sense of unease and theatricality.

Greed and competition is shown through physical contact between dancers. They fall into the space in new depths of despair and horror. Dancers shift quickly downstage, grabbing winnings as they go, they hang over the edge of stage space, hissing and spitting at the audience. They break through the fourth wall to address the audience directly; depicting Laban's image of violent, '...evil spirits of our time.'[44]

Tanzbar – Depravity

This section deals with the 'depravity'[45] set in a *Tanzbar*. Warsitz's notes mention Tango, Waltz, Foxtrot, Polka, leading us to experiment with duets involving changes in proximity, orientation, relatedness and touch. Physical contact in Waltz and Tango were considered scandalous in the 1900s, along with sexual liberation. Laban referred to:

> ... a dance of the rootless, a dance of the sick cry of the longing for lust, a dance of alluring, seductive women, a dance of greed; a chaotic quivering accompanied by crazy laughter.[46]

We worked with smooching, draping bodies, giving weight as a result of drinking and drug taking. I chose to use the same gender for some of the duets illustrating the Tanzbar images of George Grosz and Jeanne Mammen, a socio-political comment on experimental sexuality in Berlin at the time. Movement included slapping bottoms, legs open wide, sliding, touching, swaying, rocking, preening with images of lusting, raunchy, crude, sharp acrid battering Tango steps. This kind of work required the dancers to be daring. They embraced it. **5.11**

> The rottenness and decadence of our so highly praised culture stared me harshly in the face.[47]

Inspired by the research on Berlin culture at the time, I decided to create an image of a grubby bar where people go to spend their winnings, and forget the horrors of the world in which they exist. After lengthy studio investigation, I decided the female dancers would enter the scene with movement to suggest chorus lines, as vulgar entertainers, with emphasis on the pelvis, hands sliding down the body, caressing surfaces, and unfolding high leg kicks, and the men as crude, macho, strutting, potential partners.

44 Laban, 1935, p.45.
45 Laban, 1935, p.45.
46 Laban, 1935, p.42.
47 Laban, 1935, p.42.

The frivolity becomes grotesque. Repetition suggests endless chorus lines, a conveyor belt of sexual partners and the liberation of the body for sexual pleasure. Their faces are contorted, exaggerated.

Newman writes:

The interlude before the Tanzbar scene is a piece for solo piano, in the stride piano/ragtime style. This was chosen to give a bar-room feel. The piece contains a number of 'stolen-from-Bartok' flattened 5th notes in the melody, which also appeared in section 2. The overall effect was intended to be part Scott Joplin, part Jimi Hendrix. Interestingly, this section had the only musical direction from Laban himself: 'The dancers enter to a Waltz.' I ignored it.

As they choose a partner, the singer emerges, sliding up and down the side wall of the theatre. She is sultry, wearing a red silk dress with white make-up and deep red lipstick, applied rather badly, she is past her best and seedy. Close collaboration with Newman and his score, provided the direction for the singer's performances. He writes:

The piece was performed in 2010 with an opera singer. To get the character of a not very good, possibly drunk or 'high' singer, we studied Madeline Kahn's performance as Lilli von Schtupp in the film 'Blazing Saddles.' A perfect pastiche of Weimar Cabaret. In the 2011 production, as the singer had a musical theatre training, we changed the approach to one of addressing the audience more than the performers. This better achieved the effect of breaking the fourth wall and bringing the audience into the scene, engaging in, rather than witnessing the bar.

The illusion was not one of Parisian Chic, but of Berlin Cabaret, the international city of decadence where political satire was inevitable. Cabaret in Berlin was a political hotbed and not just entertainment, the scene had to show this paradox. The political nature of Newman's song, written retrospectively, was significant in the creation of the *Tanzbar* scene. I worked closely with the lyrics and rehearsed live with Newman and opera singer Catherine Carter for the 2010 recreation and again with Newman and singer Michelle Buckley for the 2011 recreation. Newman writes:

The brief for the song, was 'Funny, subversive, outrageous.' It was decided early on that it was okay to make jokes and references to later historical events, and the song could be partly looking back and summing up the whole era. I showed an early version to check that I wasn't going too far with the un-PC lyrics, and the consensus was, 'go for it'. To avoid singling out and offending any particular race, ethnicity, gender or sexual orientation, I decided to use the Frank Zappa approach and try to offend everyone.

Particular words in Newman's song prompted responses by the dancers. 'Drugs', (movement to show snorting cocaine from partner's body parts), the word 'lesbian'. (pelvic touching and thrusting), the word 'star', (hands on bottoms), the word 'skin', sliding up and down partners, the word 'Nazi' prompted the inevitable 'goose-step'. The dancers improvised within these frameworks, varying their responses in that moment.

It was a challenge to transform Carter, a polished opera singer, with little movement training, into a seedy Berlin cabaret vocalist. We experimented with the idea of the grotesque, embodying the meaning in Newman's lyrics, alternating between heavy and light qualities to show how the effects of alcohol could affect how she might hold her posture. She achieved the effect by shouting and hissing some of the lyrics rather than singing them and using the procenium wall and piano to support her weight.

Newman writes the song lyrics in full here:

A monorchid Chaplin lookalike,
Is suddenly in charge.
The world could end tomorrow
so we'd better live it large.
We decadent degenerates all congregate in bars.
I'll show you my pink triangle
If you show me
your
yellow
star.

In Berlin.
We don't care if you fit in.
Tall or short or fat or thin.
Gay straight or bi.
Or les......be..in. (sic)

In Berlin,
There's opportunity for sin,
Let me mix you a gin.
With just a microscopic amount of vermouth... in.

We'll tango
Like we're in Buenos Aires.
This town
Used to be full of fairies.
But today.
This town's full of Nazis.
Ironically they'll all retire to Argentina.
Meine shatz.

In Berlin.
It's like a book by Anaïs Nin.
Why don't you take me for a spin.
I might even show some skin.

These drinks have made me dreamy.
These powders made me dreamier.
Life was pretty sweet
In our corner of Bohemia.
You could be butch or effeminate.
It doesn't really matter
The government thinks we're ALL degenerate.

Please explain to me
Why we should invade Bulgaria.
There seems to me to be
Enough Aryans in the area.
Maybe, it's so we'll have a fighting chance.
Because Mein Gott we'll have a battle on our hands
If we try to invade France.

Monotony

Images of mass, industrial society inspired by the film *Metropolis*,[48] of utopia/dystopia and unrelenting labour and worklessness, formed the basis of *Monotony*. I considered music for this section, but conversations with Newman during rehearsals led me to trust in the power of the physical images and sound created by the dancers. **5.12**

Entrance into this scene is in silence, accompanied only by the deep grunting of the performers, to show the physicality of the action. I referred to it as 'the Worker's entrance' – the trudging, sliding of feet into the ground with the body curved over was inspired by an image by George Grosz, entitled *Arbeiter*, (Workers). Grosz's artwork depicts workers, unemployed men and vagrants in Berlin. His dark, moody style oozes dramatic potential. Further research of Bertolt Brecht's perception of Berlin was also significant.[49]

---

48 *Metropolis* is a 1927 German expressionist science-fiction film directed by Fritz Lang. Made in Germany during the Weimar Period, *Metropolis* is set in a futuristic urban dystopia, and follows the attempts of Freder, the wealthy son of the city's ruler, and Maria, whose background is not fully explained in the film, to overcome the vast gulf separating the classist nature of their city.
49 Eckardt, W.V. & Gilman,S.L. *Bertold Brecht's Berlin*, Anchor Press, New York, 1975

Images of queuing unemployed and hungry Berliners, I portrayed through group cohesion; an ordered mass giving the illusion of group unity and completeness.

Repetition is destructive to human expressivity and was used extensively in this section. Each new movement was repeated a number of times in exactly the same way. The performers' eyes are fixed, direction changes are clearly defined and rhythm change occurs without warning – it is inorganic and they appear reified. The rhythm becomes staccato, and dancers appear to be manipulated by an outside force.

This section includes work actions uncomfortable for the body, carrying heavy loads, and pushing, mechanical actions with thrusting dynamics. The movement has tension, it is bound and strong. Rehearsals were exhausting and the dancers felt the physicality and monotony of enduring long periods of repetitive work. They have to feel the dynamic tension of the body, so I encouraged them to engage with the space, to push their clenched fists into the forward dimension with resistance, keeping the movement strong, direct and sustained ending with an impact.

The dancers' vocal rhythm changes unexpectedly from hissing, to grunting, to guttural sounds, we worked to broaden vocal range by locating the dynamic of the movement in the mouth, throat and stomach.

This last scene is a juxtaposition of reification and corporeality. The repetition creates a corporeal phenomenal sequence of felt rhythm. The group have to work together to maintain the sound and spatial formation, they have to sense timing, group cohesion through acute use of spatial awareness to sustain the shape of the material. It is intensely physical and dancers require a deep commitment to the execution of this material. Cross-rhythms illustrate different parts of industry and the whole group join together in unison as they move forward downstage towards the audience. The power of this is enormous – the increasing sound while advancing forwards towards the audience is visceral.

They repeat irregular rhythms accelerating until they can no longer sustain the energy or clarity of the material. Their exhaustion is real, in the final image, they stop and stand, motionless – we see the corporeal, real people, vulnerable, desperate, exhausted. During this stillness, the audience hear the resonance of panting, breathless people. Their bodies expand and contract visibly as they breathe, an inevitable result of their physical and emotional endeavours.

Suddenly, they throw a dice to the audience with a hiss...

Blackout.

The 'evil spirits of our time' return.[50]

---

50 Laban, 1935, p.43.

Chapter Six
Recreating *Die Grünen Clowns* 1928

Green Clowns is a suite engaging with Weimar Republic culture that I recreated as a first draft in 1987. Since then the work has been honed, toured and re-recreated several times, the latest being in 2008 with Alison Curtis-Jones directing the rehearsals. Many of the photographs used in this text are from her highly praised performances with Trinity Laban dancers but the discussion here starts by tracing the life of *Die Grünen Clowns* 1928 and the realisation of *Green Clowns* 1987.

The archives of the documents surrounding the *Kammertanz Laban* activities shows a suite called *Die Grünen Clowns* performed in December 1927 and another appearing in June 1928. They did not have identical content. Three sections were the same *Gedankenflucht* (Flights of Fancy), *Zeitlupe* (Slow Motion) and *Klub der Sonderlinge* (Eccentrics' Club). I found that sometimes *Klub der Sonderlinge* appeared on its own in a *Kammertanz* evening's entertainment. It was the 1928 content that I focused on and that included the three sections common to both performances plus *Krieg* (War) *Maschine* (Machine) and *Romanze in Grün* (Romance in Green). This performance took place, directed by Dussia Bereska, on June 23rd 1928. at the 2nd Dancers' Congress this time held in Essen. **6.1** Kurt Jooss facilitated the four-day event held in the city where he ran the dance department of the Folkwang High School for the arts and the city's dance company.[1]

The performances on one evening were devoted to Chamber Dances. The other evenings covered classical dances from the opera houses of Berlin and Munich, New Russian Dance Theatre, the Mary Wigman Group, ending with Jooss's company the Essen City Dance Theatre. The evening's performance of *Kammertanz* consisted in the *Kammertanzbühne Laban* playing *Green Clowns*, sandwiched between two performances by soloists, four of them associated with Wigman, Yvonne Georgi, Harald Kreutzberg, Vera Skoronel and Gret Palucca, dancers who were beginning to make names for themselves as performers with both artistry and technique. The Laban Kammertanz clearly had serious competition in terms of the interest the performance might engender from some spectators.

The morning sessions on June 23rd were devoted to launching Choreology and Dance Notation. Laban was presenting his notation after ten years of struggle and so was a rival Vischer-Klamt (whose system was not well received). The dichotomy for the Laban circle between the topic of the

---

1 I later found a performance of *Die Grünen Clowns* dated February 1929. The programme gave a subtitle 'Comic Moves' and excluded *War, Machine* and *Romance* but added a comic man's solo and two group comedies ending with *Eccentrics' Club*.

morning, designed to enable dances to be captured in notation as scores, and the evening with the improvisation and living-in-the-moment of *Die Grünen Clowns* must have been poignant. Other sessions in the Congress focused on what dance as a theatre art might be in the present and in the future so that spectators might well be critiquing what they saw in the performances with that discourse in mind. The Chamber dance evening received little press, the *Kammertanzbühne Laban* being received as having presented 'what was expected from Laban'. So no surprises here, no controversy, no innovation.

So why did I take it on? What was commonplace in 1928, being seven years since Laban's first performances, was not commonplace in 1987 and in fact remains uncommon today. It was typical work of the Laban/Bereska collaboration and as such perfect for my purposes of refinding what the man had done.

In those early days I was at the beginning of my knowledge of Laban's choreographic methods and archeochoreology was no more than a thought. During the 1980s I had been travelling all over Europe locating evidence of Laban's professional life and come back after some two dozen trips determined to explore if it might be possible to re-find a professional dance theatre praxis that the Third Reich had succeeded in annihilating.[2]

Green Clowns was among the first of my recreations so in 1987 I was experimenting. Collaborating with me in those beginning attempts were several people with a Laban background quite different from mine. Dorothy Madden, Professor Emerita from Maryland University had started her career in Washington with choreographers and teachers who had trained with Mary Wigman. Ana Sanchez Colberg, at that point a PhD student at Laban, came from Philadelphia, trained in Wigman and Jooss techniques. The third was Stuart Hopps who started his illustrious career in the theatre with Hettie Loman, who was a mature student with Laban at the same time as myself. These three were associates I turned to during the rehearsals.

Of the six parts to the 1928 suite called *Die Grünen Clowns*, the solo *Zeitlupe* was notated as a pull-out in the first edition of the new journal *Schrittanz* published autumn 1928, this solo being the first dance to be notated. I could have reconstructed it from the score but decided against it since from what I had discovered about how Laban choreographed just to resurrect a surface form was missing the point. *Gedankenflucht* I had no knowledge of at all, none of my interviewees had spoken about it, so I could not attempt a recreation of it. With *Zeitlupe* and *Gedankenflucht* abandoned I was dealing with a suite with four sections.

For *Machine, War* and *Romance* I had enough to go on from my own studies with Laban. With the Clowns photographs I could attempt the *Eccentrics'*

2 Our attempts in 1987 were filmed and the footage is available at Trinity Laban Archive. The DVD *Laban Dance Works* published in 1990 contains short extracts of the *Kammertanz* of the 1920s together with some takes of those first recreations.

Club. From the images it seemed that the number of performers was not constant which confirmed my belief that Laban used whoever was available or whoever had a dance in their body memory at the time. Casting has changed over the times that I have recreated this work. I have notes for a cast of thirteen in the performance with Transitions Dance Company in Volgograd, Curtis-Jones had more in her recreation in 2008. The piece is so choreographed that numbers are not crucial at all, nor is gender, provided there is one man and one woman for the Romance.

The fact that two very different suites were danced, 1927 and 1928, suggested that each section was independent and could be danced in this suite or that. What I knew must be in place in a Laban suite was different kinds of theatre to enable the spectator to have a varied experience. I started with *Machine*. Laban's attitude to industrialisation is well known, He distrusted it and was deeply concerned that mechanisation dehumanised the person. His statements as a military cadet made his attitude clear. That concern was the idea behind the piece.

Many machine dances existed in the 1920s. Many were representational asking dancers to perform machine-like movements but I knew that that was not his purpose. When Laban took me on as an apprentice he sent me to Pilkingtons Tile factory where he was employed by a team of management consultants to increase production. There I experienced first-hand what it was like to work on the assembly line repeating all day an eleven second action sequence compressing sand into tile. It was Time that the operatives were working against, each was timed by an official with a stopwatch intent on getting them to work faster. My job was to write in detailed notation what movements operatives actually did. I was to inform Laban where the points of physical stress were in the sequence. That convinced me that in *Machine* discomfort and time should dominate the dancers and for the audience to appreciate that, time must be audible through a beat. While it might have been a drum beat or piano in 1928 I turned to Adda Heynssen's keyboard piece entitled *Machine Rhythms* to be played at a pace uncomfortably fast for the dancers. I felt that I had come as near as I could get with this musical choice because in the Foreword to the 1945 publication of Heynssen's *Music for Modern Dance* Laban wrote:

> I have had the great pleasure of working over the years with Miss Heynssen and watched with interest her many successes in international dance congresses.

Dorothy Madden solved the problem of how to embody 'conveyor belt' by putting the dancers on all fours, one cheek on the backside of the dancer ahead, lurching, ratching forward, taking turns to scramble on hands and feet over the dancer ahead and so progress across stage. It was awkward, the dancers unused to this kind of discomfort were disconcerted. The movement had a natural rhythm that was not regular but the dancers had to make it conform to the musical beat, a pounding 6/8. **6.2** Charlie Chaplin's satirical performance of an operative caught up in machinery was a well-known cinema image but I needed to get the discomfort not as a comedy but as a feeling of tension that the audience could, with empathy, pick up.

I used the Pilkington's tile-making sequence for the second motif, exaggerating the moments of stress. The dancers 'scoop sand' with their left arm into a mould in from of them, their wrists having to arch to get it onto the right spot. With their right hand they grasp a stick and in a speedy to and fro motion flatten the sand as fast as possible and immediately reach up for a handle uncomfortably high, pulling it down with force and holding it there while their left leg steps far forward on to a pedal that raises the mould so that handle and pedal counter-press the sand. The dynamic then changes as fingers and thumbs lift the delicate tile on to the conveyor belt for transport to the kiln. The operatives performed this sequence all day, everyday, year on year. The stress, the boredom, the dehumanisation was palpable. That is what I had to get the dancers to feel.

As the piece progresses the stress gets out of hand and disoriented until the dancers become objects conveyed, this way and that, along a juddering belt. We watched a film clip of milk bottles tottering on their way from cow to cup and rehearsed turn, totter, turn, totter, turn, totter in sharp formation. They spin off line, caught into the conveyor belt and lurch cross stage to exit.

The image of dehumanisation is enhanced in *Green Clowns* by a white face mask, white swimming cap covering every inch of hair and a dull green dungaree-type garment. They are faceless, genderless, ageless. Being full face and with only small eye and nostril holes the mask is problematic. Both vision and breath is inhibited but expressively the mask is a powerful feature.

Section two is *Krieg* (War). **6.3** Having worked as a student with Laban and Ullmann on a piece entitled *Chaos, Fight and Liberation* I had a good idea how this section was built up. The relationship signs in the notation were the clue, together with his studies of non-verbal communication. Facing, moving towards, moving away, arriving at, passing, being near, surrounding, touching, sliding, supporting the weight of, and so on these are the syllables that *War* is made of. **6.4** What is also there is a dynamic focus from behaviour. As you come near with an accelerating impactive dynamic it reads as aggressive. Turning sharply to face reads of catching the other unawares, invading their space with a thrusting elbow reads as pugnacious. Every time *War* is recreated the whole scene is built up of pairs approaching, relating, and retreating, geographically organised in the space, and staggered in time, increasing in pace and vehemence and technical daring.**6.5** Each couple works on the structures given them, using their ingenuity to find a way to turn a task into a personal statement, contrasting high with low, connecting arm with foot, knee with head, tossing with grabbing, piercing with floundering, feeling the development from casual rudeness to purposeful murder. As they sense a climax they freeze with a shout from one of them 'ENOUGH', 'GENUG', their shortage of breath is genuine and heard. War exhausts.

The tempo and duration of the scene are unique to each performance. The dancers' breath that crescendos into shouts and cries as the scene progresses is the music. *War* is fearful to perform. The dancers find the masks a severe problem that they learn to tolerate over time. It is essential to rehearse in them.

The Procession of the Dying People is captured in a 1928 photograph. **6.6** You can see that they are progressing to the left, they are helping each other, holding hands, supporting each other. One can construe all manner of trace forms that their gestures have made as they move into the tableau. It constitutes a typical Laban group canon based on individual improvisation that is edited and rehearsed to create a polykinetic hymn of despair. The well known image of *The Dance of Death* by Hans Holbein, 'a masterpiece of the macabre' has been the inspiration of several dances and was here. In Jooss's *The Green Table* the cast follow the triumphal figure of Death while here there is no triumph, simply pathos.

The procession is created by a canon. **6.7** Each performer has one telling movement phrase, an impulsive response to being mortally wounded, in face, in gut, in flank, in knees followed by a slow motion reaction as their life force gradually ebbs away. Then they function as a canon, passing on their phrase to another dancer. My note of the canon is for a cast of twelve. There is no music, a sound emanates with each dancer's sharp intake of breath and long fading sigh, overlapping one after another.

Romanze in Grün is a duo, a romantic duet with the rest of the Clowns observing and commenting as the relationship unfolds. **6.8** It appeared from the programme that each section of the suite stood, just one of four, but very soon a connection between the sections emerged. From my notes of one recreation I wrote:

> This is a duo asking the question, is it possible that people can love each other again after such hatred? Across ethnic barriers?

If I recall this note was made at the time of the Balkans genocide, Serb against Bosnian, centred on Herzegovina and Sarajevo. It was not difficult for the dancers to relate their present with the dance they were creating, two innocent lovers caught in the emotional cross fire of prejudice. How real would that have been for the *Kammertanzers* with the reminders of WWI on every street corner. For the surrounding Clowns I wrote:

> The Clowns are a chorus commenting on the emerging romance with a mix of hope, shock, excitement, negation. Each Clown can react according to his own

observations and feeling to reflect the problems of post-war reconciliation.

The duo itself is made in the same way as *War*, through the structures in relationship signs in the notation. Here the dynamics are quite different, starting with bound tentative flow as the two dancers become aware of each other, hesitant. Their masks are removed and we see a young woman and a young man. As it develops from approach, near, touch, support, surround, et al, the dynamic increases gradually until small-size impulsive flow begins to emerge and the couple's contact becomes more all-embracing demanding more technical daring. Curtis-Jones rehearsed four duos. each distinct and with the dancers' input, but all four made from the same detailed relationship structures.

Midway through 'partial support' is the structure, a weight-sharing move with huge potential for expressivity. How much trust is developing between the lovers? Is there reluctance to give your weight that your timing can convey? The dancers come to realise the subtlety that they are capable of as they watch each other's interpretation. One has his palm supporting her shoulder, another has his lower arms supporting her back, another has his outstretched fist supporting her forehead.

There is music. It has varied but always centred on a female voice, or flute or oboe improvising on a melody, improvised by Annie Gillespie at the first recreation. Annie wrote it down and I have used it as a basis ever since, just as the *Kammertanzers* spontaneously sang a theme for the Moon in performances of *Himmel und Erde*. Here the singer follows the ebb and flow, hesitation and ecstasy as the romance takes its course. It can be a moving piece, made poignant as the relationship founders, she closes in on herself, the chorus melts away, leaving the young man alone, but it depends on the sensitivity coming from the soul of the soloists and chorus, to make it work as an Expressionist Romance.

The Eccentrics Club is another kind of theatre altogether. The 1928 photograph is the clue to the action. **6.9** In small behavioural gestures they are acting eccentrically, kissing, poking, scratching each other. Laban refers to the piece like this:

> One of my solos Caprice and also the group play The Cranks' Club, which later formed a basis for our dance suite The Green Clowns, were reminiscent of the images of The Night.[3]

So there is a dark side to these eccentric and cranky people. Following one of the photographs, I have their faces revealed for this scene. They enter like this, from my notes:

> Unison over-exaggerated, a canon entry cross stage. Goose step, loud kisses, a 'no no no' finger shake, teeter on tiptoe, 'tut tut'. Definite sound counterpoint from

---

3 Laban, 1935, p.109.

the feet, kisses, the no nos and the tut tuts.

They gather in a close group, back to the audience, pause, one starts to scratch herself, picked up by the others until a mayhem of scratching each other in all manner of places develops. Out of it for no reason whatever a leader jumps out with a rousing cry, progresses cross stage, the Clowns following like thoughtless sheep, another jumps out with a counter cry, they change direction and follow him like sheep, and repeat. We call it the 'I'm the best politician follow me' motif. It resonates as a pastiche of the tyrant in *Gaukelei* but here they are upstart, pathetic would-be tyrants. In motif three they gather in small groups and engage in loud licking, poking, shaking, rudely. **6.10** One Clown emerges to spit loudly and gutterally (in the quality of *Les Fauves*) whereupon they fall to the ground and spin round and round for no reason and jump up one at a time presenting their particular eccentric personality in voice and motion. They end advancing in a cross stage line haranguing the audience with discourse on current affairs, from landladies to the government, whatever they choose, advancing from up stage to down stage with assertive and profound gestures.

Green Clowns has great theatricality. Audiences love it because it incites thought, a lump in the throat, astonishment, merriment. Remembering what Laban said about audiences being more than buyers and consumers and artists being more than egocentric dreamers:

> We are all one, and what is at stake is the universal soul out of which and for which we have to create.[4]

Curtis-Jones took this scenario on in 2008, twenty years after my first production. I asked her about her experience.

1.How did the War Memorial come about? What did you want to get from it?

I felt the ending of 'War' was such a significant moment in the work that it required a greater tribute to capture the poignancy of this. The scene builds momentum through increasing speed and force. It has intense physical material involving advancing, retreating, contact and loud vocalisation of strong, impactive dynamic energy. It ends with one dancer shouting '*Enough!*' followed by silence and stillness. I wanted to develop the resonance of this and to find a way to conclude this scene and to provide an introduction to the next scene 'Dying Procession'. In earlier versions of 'War' by Preston-Dunlop, dancers find a body shape to show victory or hope. I used this as a source, with one dancer reaching into the space while the remaining dancers observe, and developed the idea further by drawing the dancers slowly together in close proximity to create a group tableau.**6.11**

4 Laban. 1935. p. 94.

They reach into the space using spatial projection, the tableau is not just a shape in stillness, but more about projecting energy through the general space and beyond. I was inspired by the American War Memorial Iwo Jima in Arlington, America... its scale, (I was dwarfed by it), and how the soldiers' postures replicate the physicality of placing the flag in the ground. I used Laban's theory of Harmonic Opposition to shape the tableau.

This extension of energy to the extremes of the space, gives the dancers a counter tension pull from sky to earth for the beginning of Dying Procession. They all breathe in at the furthest point so they can release it to vocalise the long outward breath of the dying... the beginning of Dying Procession.

2. You rehearsed four duos for Romance. Tell me about them.

I set up the improvisation tasks for Romance so that all group members were involved in creating a duet. I then selected four duos, all unique, for each performance, and worked closely with them to refine the material. To encourage relationships, I explored proxemics (nearness and distance) and touch. In this scene, the remaining dancers become observers, and are placed on stage, in various 3-ring spatial formations, to create a 'Clown Chorus'. The clowns express their reactions based on observations of the duet. These vary with each performance contributing to the 'liveness' of the event and creating a new surface form with each performance, sympathetic to Laban's idea of temporality. I worked closely with opera singer Catherine Carter to create an intimacy for the scene. We rehearsed so that she could also respond to what she saw in the duets, following the movement rather than the movement being dictated to by the sound, making her voice soar and fall through sensitive changes in pitch and volume. Her responses varied in each performance and gave the dancers a phenomenal experience.

3 What did you work on in Club?

We had great fun with 'Club of the Eccentric People'. Dancers had to find moments of absurd behaviour to show eccentricities of people. This required daring to indulge in movement which, to some, might be embarrassing. They had to believe and trust in their responses. Our work as a close collaborative group, by this stage in the process, gave them enormous confidence, they were afraid of nothing.

The scene opens with loud kisses, 'tut tutting', and use of the word 'no' counterpointing the rhythmic pattern of the feet, a marked contrast to the intimate quiet of the 'Romance' section before. We found humour in mundane behaviour such as scratching and made references to more recent comic performers of movement (John Cleese and silly walks). 'Club' shows the absurdity of the masses following those in power. One dancer leads on a particular trajectory and the others follow, replicating their ridiculous sound and movement patterns.

The most difficult co-ordinated activity came at the end of the piece, where the performers executed complex rhythmic patterns involving a stepping pattern moving forward in unison in one rhythm, while gesturing using another rhythm and speaking simultaneously in another... I asked them to speak out about the political climate and issues that felt really important to them. Their voices and gestures became animated and rhythmically complex because they were so engaged... this was challenging for even the most experienced of our performers and took hours of rehearsal to achieve the sense of group cohesion while maintaining their individuality.

4 How did you get a strong cohesion as a group for the dancers?

Laban's intention to remove music and a set vocabulary of steps to reveal the medium is well known. Much of *Green Clowns* is performed in silence and is not set to a specific time frame. As the work is largely structured improvisation and the surface form not entirely 'fixed', this encourages acute awareness and sensitivity to others in performance. The performer's responses were immediate in performance time and space and the work as a whole varied with each performance as a result. This takes courage and daring, the feeling of unpredictability keeps the phenomenal aliveness and the creative nature of the work ongoing. It becomes a temporal event. 'They got me to pay attention every single minute. I wanted to know what happened next.' (Mary Ann Hushlak, February, 2008)

Laban's esoteric and spiritual concerns were referred to throughout as a background to his view of the world, which we needed to understand. The dancers experienced moving as a group, of experiencing togetherness and the complexity of moving in unison... 'living in harmony with nature and the cosmos', we connected with the outside by dancing outside, just as Laban did with his dancers. Writer Mary Ann Hushlak comments; 'What also really impressed me was how the students worked as an ensemble. It wasn't just that they put their hearts and souls into it, but all their energy and worked as a team. I remember being in Berlin after the Wall came down but before unification; we went to Bertolt Brecht's theatre to see the Berliner Ensemble do *Mother Courage and her Children*. The sense of ensemble acting I saw there was palpable in the students' work here. You felt as if they were united' (February, 2008). Janet Lunn comments: 'there is a tangible connection and sensitivity between each and every dancer on the stage throughout the dance'. (Volume 27, No2 Summer 2008)

During rehearsals I challenged them to keep the group sensitivity but to find their own experience of movement, '... namely to enhance their own inner light.' (Laban, 1975, p.137) It is interesting to note, that by shifting their focus, (their 'inner attitude'), they could transform how they engaged with their movement material and how this, along with their energy and enthusiasm was paramount in the success of recreating the work. I avoided dividing the group, or selecting individual dancers to work on tasks at the expense of excluding others. Over time they became very connected in the pursuit of generating and embodying material. The group worked on every creative task together and began spending time together outside rehearsals, helping to establish a sense of 'community' to which Laban often refers. In technique classes, I encouraged repetition of movement in unison, not only to find the intricacies and detail in the material but to experience a strong sense of group cohesion.

5. What is the value of recreating an expressionist work for the dancers?

My personal research interest is investigating the value of revisiting and re-creating historic work for today's dance artist, and how as an artist researcher, practical investigation and dialogue with the past can inform artists of the future.

Is Laban's expressionist work relevant today? Absolutely – but it is the approach of Laban the artist/researcher, a spirit of enquiry, and an ability to adapt to the changing needs of our aspiring dancers, that is necessary in order to make the work accessible.

Through this collaboration, dancers learnt what 'performative' means in practice, how the movement 'speaks'; how it engages with the audience, not just how it is felt as a proprioceptive experience for the performer. They had to feel the movement, a very different experience to just 'doing' the movement, they had to find a performance truth, an honesty in their engagement with the material. Expressivity was achieved through clarity of their performance intention; that is, understanding their movement choices both spatially and dynamically and developing the ability to make those choices visible to the audience. Their spatial accuracy was enhanced through their choreutic knowledge and rhythmic decisions requiring knowledge of effort qualities were also developed.

The dancers entered into the spirit of the work; its expressivity, freedom of movement, sometimes simply moving for the sheer pleasure of movement and not concerning themselves necessarily, with 'placement'.

The performance challenges and skills they needed to perform *Green Clowns* became apparent to them very early in the recreation process. The challenge of using masks meant they had to work in a particular way to allow the body to 'speak' expressively. Their movement intention required

TANZFESTSPIELE
ESSEN 1928
Samstag, den 23. Juni 1928, 20 Uhr

MITWIRKENDE:

Edgar Frank / Yvonne Georgi / Harold Kreutzberg / Lucienne Lamballe / Palucca / Vera Skoronel
Kammertanzbühne Laban

1.	Palucca	In leichter Bewegung
2.	Lamballe	Klassische Variationen auf einen Walzer von Chopin (Choreographie: Egorowda)
3.	Georgi-Kreutzberg	Persisches Lied
4.	Skoronel	Freudentanz
5.	Palucca	Gebundene Ruhe
6.	Frank	Slavische Rhythmen

II.

7 Kammertanzbühne L A B A N , Leitung: Dussia Bereska.

„DIE GRÜNEN CLOWNS" Choreographie: Dussia Bereska.
Maschine (Musik von E. I. Kahn)
Krieg
Zeitlupe
Romanze in Grün
Gedankenflucht
Klub der Sonderlinge

MITWIRKENDE:

Dussia Bereska / Carola Dessauer / Rosemarie Gerig / Kurt Graff / Werner Hermann / Herbert Hirlinger
Susanne Kabitz / Fritz Klingenbock / Robert Robst / Heinz Rosenthal / Elinor Warsitz

III

8.	Georgi	Mazurka
9.	Kreutzberg	Spanischer Tanz
10	Lamballe	Pizzicati
11.	Frank	Rhapsodie nègre
12.	Skoronel	Tanz des wilden Gottes
13.	Palucca	Technische Improvisationen vom Musiker und der Tänzerin im Augenblick frei improvisiert
14.	Georgi-Kreutzberg	Groteske Tanzszenen

Es begleiten am Flügel: Nr. 1, 5, 13 Herbert Trantow / Nr. 2, 10 Herbert Kleiner / Nr. 3, 8, 9, 14 Friedrich Wildans
Nr. 4, 12 Hedwig Scherler / Nr. 6 und 11 Rudi Vollrath und Nr. 7 Rudolf Wagner-Régeny.

6.1 Dance Festival Programme at the Second Dancers' Congress, Essen.

6.2 *Green Clowns 2008 Machine*.
Photographer Kyle Stevenson.

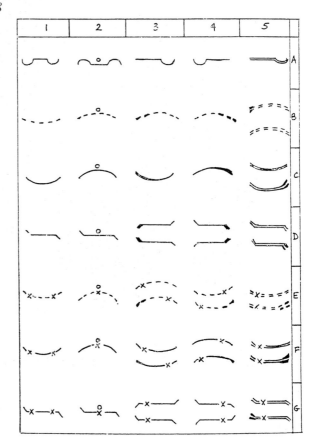

6.3 Relationship structures used in *War* and *Romance*.

6.4 *Green Clowns* 1987. *War* scene. Photographer Tony Nandi.

6.5 *Green Clowns* 1987, *War* scene. Photographer Tony Nandi.

6.6 *Die Grünen Clowns, The Procession of the Dying*, 1928.
Photographer Wide World, Broschet & Co.

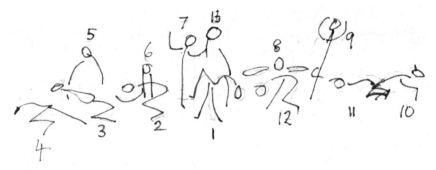

6.7 Plan of the canon for 12 dancers, *Procession of the Dying* in *Green Clowns.*

6.8 *Green Clowns* 1989, duo in *Romance*. Photographer Tony Nandi.

6.9 *Die Grünen Clowns 1928, Club of the Eccentrics.*

6.10 *Die Grünen Clowns 1929, Club of the Eccentrics.*

6.11 *Green Clowns 2009*, War Memorial. Photographer Kyle Stevenson.

greater sophistication than they had anticipated in order to communicate the themes and moods of the piece.

As an educator and an artist, I have seen how the dancers have been transformed by this process. They claim that as a result of this experience, they have developed as performers and have re-connected with dance as a performative art form. They have remembered why it is they chose to dance in the first place... to communicate, to express, to engage and for the pleasure of moving. Each in turn identified that the skills learned were transferable to all areas of their training; analysis, choreographic practice, technical training and performance.

Melanie Clarke, choreographer, lecturer at Trinity Laban, wrote:

> I think through (Green Clowns) everyone's perception of Laban as an Artist and innovator has shifted up, because we were so moved and engaged in this recreation. (February, 2008)

Dancer Jamie Roberts wrote:

> I know now from experiencing this form of technique I have found the joy in dancing again and have learnt that this pioneer's works and theories can be used to enhance our other techniques and ways of thinking about dance. (February 2008)

Alison Curtis-Jones

Conclusion

The recent recreations discussed in this book, and available to view as DVDs, are at different stages of the recreation continuum. *Die Grünen Clowns* has been recreated several times since the first draft in the late 1980s, in productions and in workshops. In 1990 it closed a programme consisting in *Dithyrambus* (a dynamic group opener), *Orchidée, Krystall, Marotte and Mondäne*, (solos) *Marsch* (the comic quartet) and *Oben und Unten* (the satiric ensemble piece) and the evening was toured in the UK.

At that time the parameters of the discourse on recreation, reconstruction, archeochoreology were only beginning. I was learning what it takes to get hold of the essentials of a work thought to be lost. Since then all manner of engagements with the dance heritage have been undertaken by other scholars and choreographers some of which are discussed in the paper 'Gained in Translation', by Leslie-Anne Sayers and myself.[1] In that first attempt in the 1980s I concentrated on the casting, putting together a company with the mix of gender and age that mirrored the make up of the *Kammertanzbühne Laban*. We ranged from nineteen-year-old students to mature professionals. I set up a rehearsal schedule that mirrored the situation of the 1920s, with an expressionist technique class taking place on the grass outside, with the 'company' contributing to the choreography.

Since then *Green Clowns*, as it is known today, has been mounted on Transitions Dance Company, been taken to Volgograd, had workshop performances in Tokyo, Beijing, Rio de Janiero and several in the UK. The experience of different cast sizes and theatres, different purposes, different audiences, has enabled Alison Curtis-Jones and I to hone the recreation processes of *Clowns* in much the way Laban and Bereska did in the 1920s, suiting the work to the occasion. While I have mounted the *Kammertanz Solos and Duos* on several occasions *Nacht* has had only two recreations both by Curtis-Jones. In the original and the recent performances the work was rehearsed for a company of over twenty dancers but this autumn Alison Curtis-Jones will present a version of it for six dancers for performance in the small Teatro San Materno in Ascona with Oli Newman adapting the score for the smaller stage and casting. *Der Schwingende Tempel* has had only one recreation so far so must be regarded as practical research in progress.

What has made the thirty-year project worthwhile beyond expectations has been the reaction by the participating dancers and the surprised spectators. The dancers' experience has shifted from being curious in the 1980s to one that can only be described as profound recently. They embraced

---

1 Preston-Dunlop, V. and Sayers, L-A. 'Gained in Translation: Recreation as Critical Practice'. *Dance Chronicle* 34, 5-45, 2011 Routledge.

with overwhelming enthusiasm the demands of expressionism and Laban's creative method. Apparently working that way feels neither old-fashioned nor outmoded but a refreshing change. Dancers reported interest in dealing with topics that seemed to retain relevance to their lives. They had great interest in the supporting technical training, provided by Curtis-Jones and Clarke, with its colossal physical demands and daring that nevertheless took account of their personal physique and their capacity to intend. They welcomed a choreographic method that demanded imaginative, meaningful and witty improvisation, where their individual movement voice was welcomed and developed through a directorial method that was collaborative. By using identifiable structural elements the dancers could work themselves to transform their improvised drafts into material. The whole process, they reported, was empowering. They welcomed the living-in-the-moment uncertainty of performing when the timing was open to group decisions. They welcomed the demand for facial expression that was then choreographed, sound making and speaking/shouting/laughing that expanded their normal range of expressivity.

As for the spectators they have greeted the performances with enthusiastic applause and genuine interest, according to the post-performance chatter in the bar. In our recreations the scenes are more concise than in the original partly to take account of the shorter attention span of today's consumer culture than that of the 1920s. The performances appear to have drawn the spectator in giving rise to an array of experiences. Laban's respect for his audiences seems to have been embodied in his works through his attention to what a theatrical event is. 'Diversity' was his watchword for what he offered. As an example *Green Clowns* shifts with each short scene from promoting attention, curiosity, awe, surprise, compassion, amusement, shock and hilarity. Each scene offers a balance of phenomenal and semiotic experience, what Bert States called the binocular vision of theatre. Laban and Bereska, and we as recreators, set out to satisfy the desire for meaning that many spectators have as well as giving them the surprise that expressionist performance is.

There is much still to discover about Laban's theatre works as further recreations are attempted but also much on how we, as a dance community, engage with our rich and varied heritage. In the fervour to make new events and forge new genres choreography can be 'a forgetful art', as historian Martin Hargreaves put it in the documentary on *The Swinging Temple*.

Bibliography

Dörr, E. *Rudolf von Laban: Leben und Werk des Künsters, 1979-1936.* Unpublished PhD thesis, 1999. Extended in *Rudolf Laban: The Dancer of the Crystal*, translation assistants Lori Ann Lantz, Amy J. Klemment. Plymouth: Scarecrow Press, 2008.

Duncan, A. *Art Nouveau.* London: Thames and Hudson, 1994.

Eckardt, W.V. & Gilman, S. L. *Bertold Brecht's Berlin.* New York: Anchor Press, 1975.

Hart-Davis, D. *Hitler's Games, The 1936 Olympics.* London: Century, 1986.

Jaques-Dalcrose, E. 'How to revive dancing (1912)' in *Rhythm, Music and Education.* Woking: The Dalcrose Society, 1921.

Izerghina, A. *Henri Matisse; Paintings and Sculptures in Soviet Museums.* Leningrad: Aurora Art Publishers, 1978.

Kandinsky, W. Trans. Sadler, M.T.H. *Concerning the Spiritual in Art.* New York: Dover Publications, 1977.

Laban, R. *Ein Leben für den Tanz*, 1935. Trans. Lisa Ullmann as *A Life for Dance.* London: Macdonald and Evans, 1975.

Laban, R. Letters from Laban to Suzanne Perrottet, 1912- 13. Trans. Simone Michelle. Laban Collection. Trinity Laban.

Laban, R. ed. L. Ullmann. *Choreutics.* London: McDonald &Evans, 1966.

Lloyd, Jill. *German Expressionism, Primitivism and Modernity.* New Haven: Yale University Press, 1991.

Lucie-Smith, E. *Symbolist Art.* London: Thames and Hudson, 1972.

Lenman, R. Politics and Culture: The State and the Avant-Garde in Munich 1886-1914. in Evans, R. L. ed. *Society and Politics in Wilhelmine Germany.* London: Croom Helm, 1978.

Maletic, V. *Body Space Expression.* Berlin: Mouton de Gruyter, 1987.

McCaw, D. ed. *The Laban Sourcebook.* London: Routledge, 2011.

McIntosh, C. *The Rosicrucians.* Boston: Weiser Books, 1998.

Peukert D. J. K. Trans. Deveson, R. *The Weimar Republic.* London: Penguin Books, 1993.

Parat, P. *An Artist Against the Third Reich, Ernst Barlach 1933-1938.* Cambridge: Cambridge University Press, 2003.

Pollig, H. ed. *Prints and Drawings of the Weimar Republic.* Stuttgart: Institute for Foreign Cultural Relations and Authors. 1987.

Preston-Dunlop, V. *Rudolf Laban: An Extraordinary Life.* London: Dance Books, 1998.

Preston-Dunlop, V. and Carlisle, A. *Living Architecture*, DVD. London: Verve Publishing, 2008.

Preston-Dunlop, V. & Sayers, L. A. 'Gained in Translation: Recreation as Creative Practice', *Dance Chronicle*, 34. Routledge, 2011.

Preston-Dunlop, V. *Point of Departure*. London: Verve Publishing, 2001.

Richter, H. Trans. Britt, D. *Dada Art and Anti-Art*. New York: Oxford University Press, 1978.

Schlee, A. Trans as 'At the turning point of the New Dance'. *Schrifttanz* Vol. III. no. 1, April 1930, in Preston-Dunlop, V. and Lahusen, S. eds. *Schrifttanz: A View of German Dance in the Weimar Republic*. London: Dance Books, 1990.

Steiner, R. *A Lecture on Eurhythmy*. London: Anthroposophical Publishing Co, 1926.

Schlemmer, T. ed. *The Letters and Diaries of Oskar Schlemmer*. Evaston: N W University Press, 1990.

Walther, V. Rudolf von Laban, Reigenspiele by his Tanzbühne on 14th, 17th 18th December 1922 in Herbert Grainer-Mai, ed. *Freund und Feind: Kritiken aus Fünf Jahrzehnten*. Weimar und Leipzig, 1980.

Weiss, P. *Kandinsky in Munich: The Formative Jugendstil Years*. Princeton: Princeton University Press, 1979.

Willett, J. *The New Sobriety, 1917-33*. London: Thames and Hudson, 1978.

Wilmshurst, W.L. *The Meaning of Masonry*. New York: Barnes and Noble, 1999.

Wigman, M. 'Rudolf Labans Lehre vom Tanz'. *Die neue Schaubühne*, Sept. 1921.

Wolfensberger, Giorgio, J. ed. *Suzanne Perrottet: Ein Bewegtes Leben*, Bern: Benteli Verlag. undated (1990).

Index